Get ready to write!

Color and draw to finish the picture.

Write sentences about your picture.

Check your work.

COMPLETE THE SCENE
FUN SENTENCE WRITING FOR KIDS

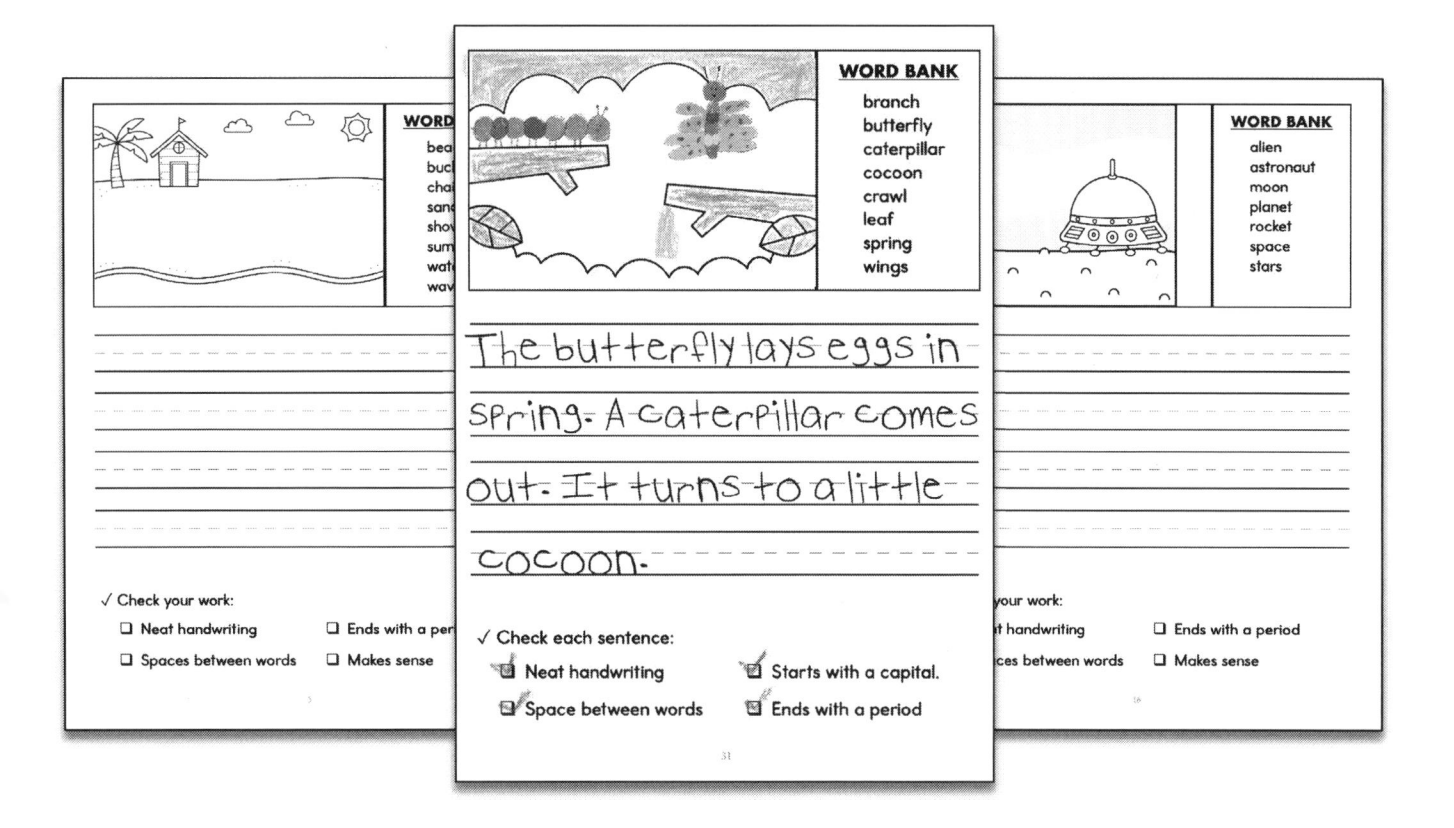

How to Use This Book

It's hard to practice writing when you can't think of something to write about. But this workbook will give your child all kinds of fun ideas!

Each page features a background scene accompanied by a word bank. Your child can draw and color to complete the scene any way they want. Then, use the word bank and lines below to write their own sentences about the picture.

At the bottom of each page is a short checklist that prompts kids to look over their writing and make sure it's their best work.

This workbook will let your child's imagination run wild, inspire creative thinking, and provide opportunities for lots of fun sentence-writing practice!

© Fishyrobb 2024-present All rights reserved.

Copyright © 2024 Janet Ecochardt - Fishyrobb

All rights reserved. No part of this publication may be reproduced, distributed, or transmitted in any form or by any means, including photocopying, recording, or other electronic or mechanical methods, without the prior written permission of the author, except in the case of classroom use and certain other noncommercial uses permitted by copyright law.

Contact the author :
fishyrobb.com

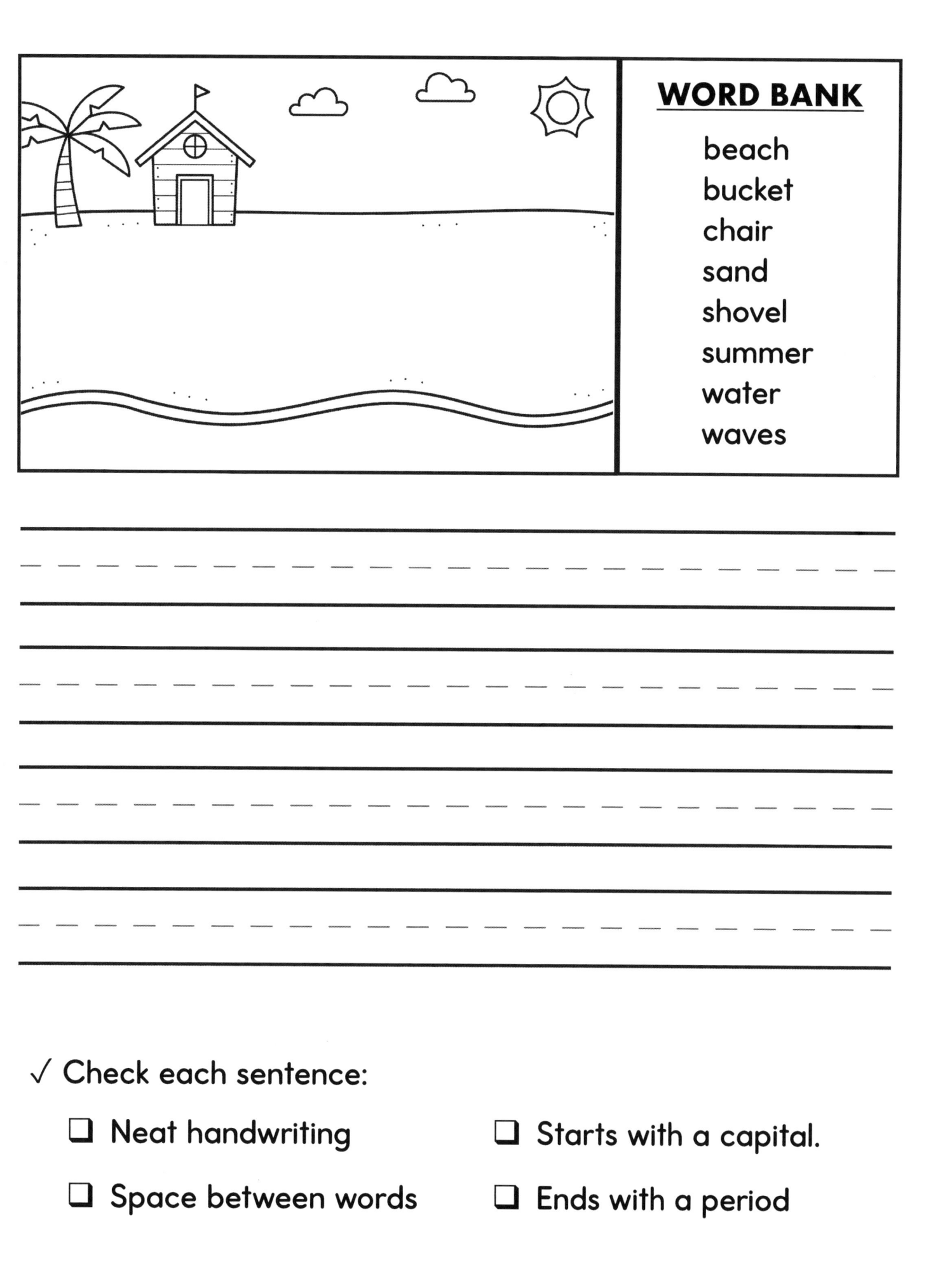

WORD BANK

beach
bucket
chair
sand
shovel
summer
water
waves

✓ Check each sentence:

❑ Neat handwriting   ❑ Starts with a capital.

❑ Space between words   ❑ Ends with a period

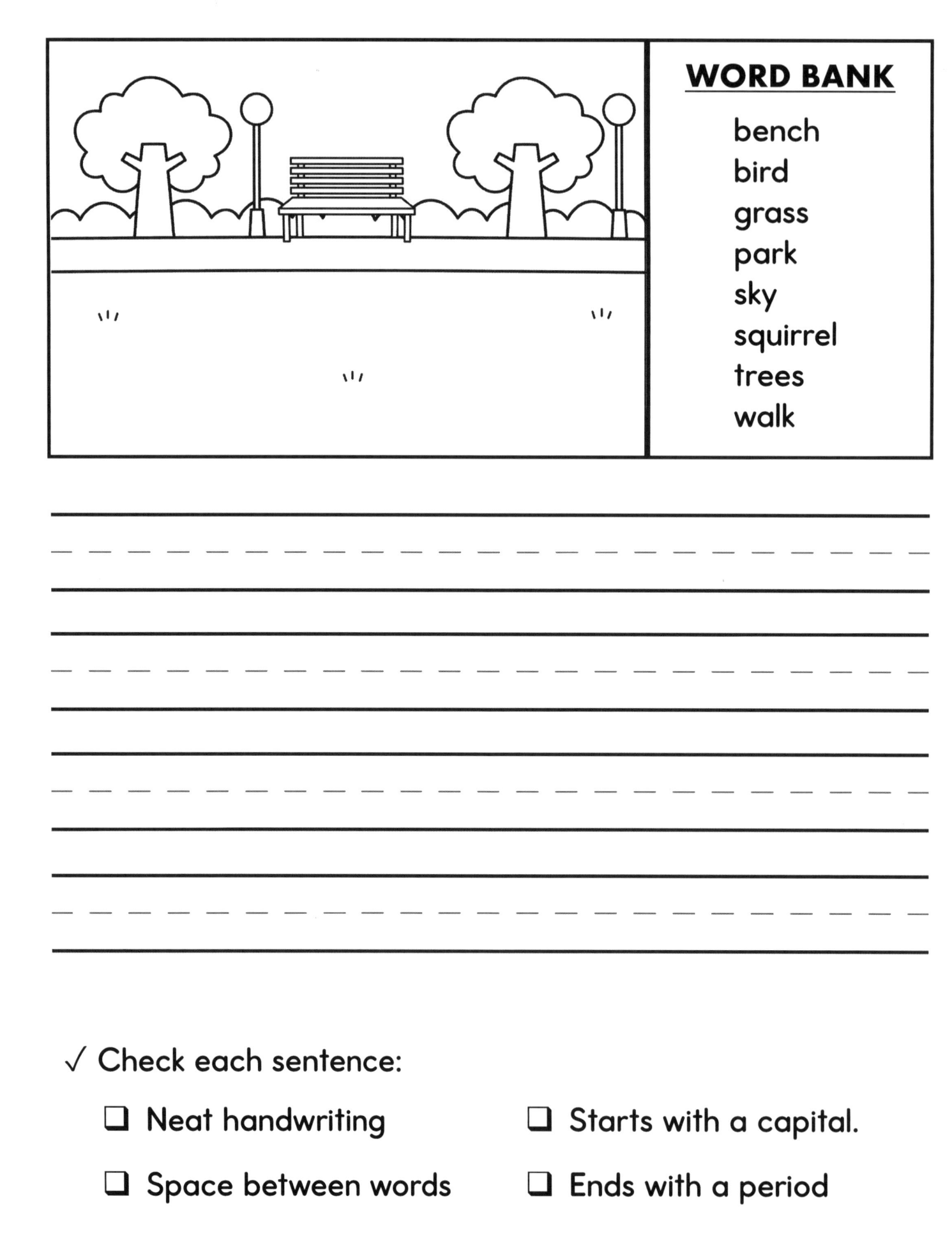

WORD BANK

bench
bird
grass
park
sky
squirrel
trees
walk

✓ Check each sentence:

❑ Neat handwriting ❑ Starts with a capital.

❑ Space between words ❑ Ends with a period

WORD BANK

birthday
cake
candles
decorate
invite
party
presents

✓ Check each sentence:

❏ Neat handwriting ❏ Starts with a capital.

❏ Space between words ❏ Ends with a period

WORD BANK

canoe
fishing
paddle
path
river
trees
woods

✓ Check each sentence:

❏ Neat handwriting ❏ Starts with a capital.

❏ Space between words ❏ Ends with a period

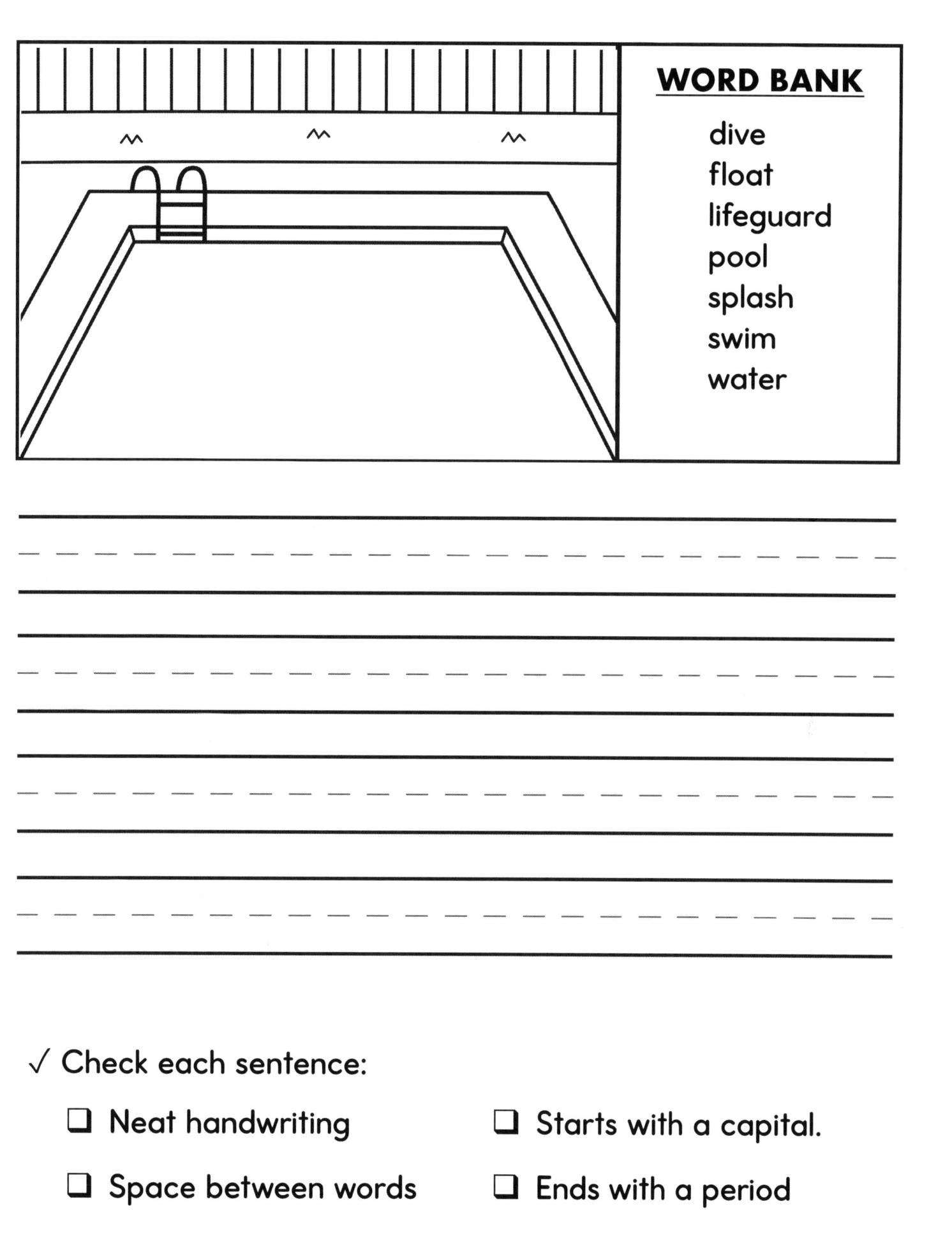

WORD BANK

dive
float
lifeguard
pool
splash
swim
water

✓ Check each sentence:

❏ Neat handwriting ❏ Starts with a capital.

❏ Space between words ❏ Ends with a period

WORD BANK

animals
circus
clown
food
games
show
tent

✓ Check each sentence:

❑ Neat handwriting   ❑ Starts with a capital.

❑ Space between words   ❑ Ends with a period

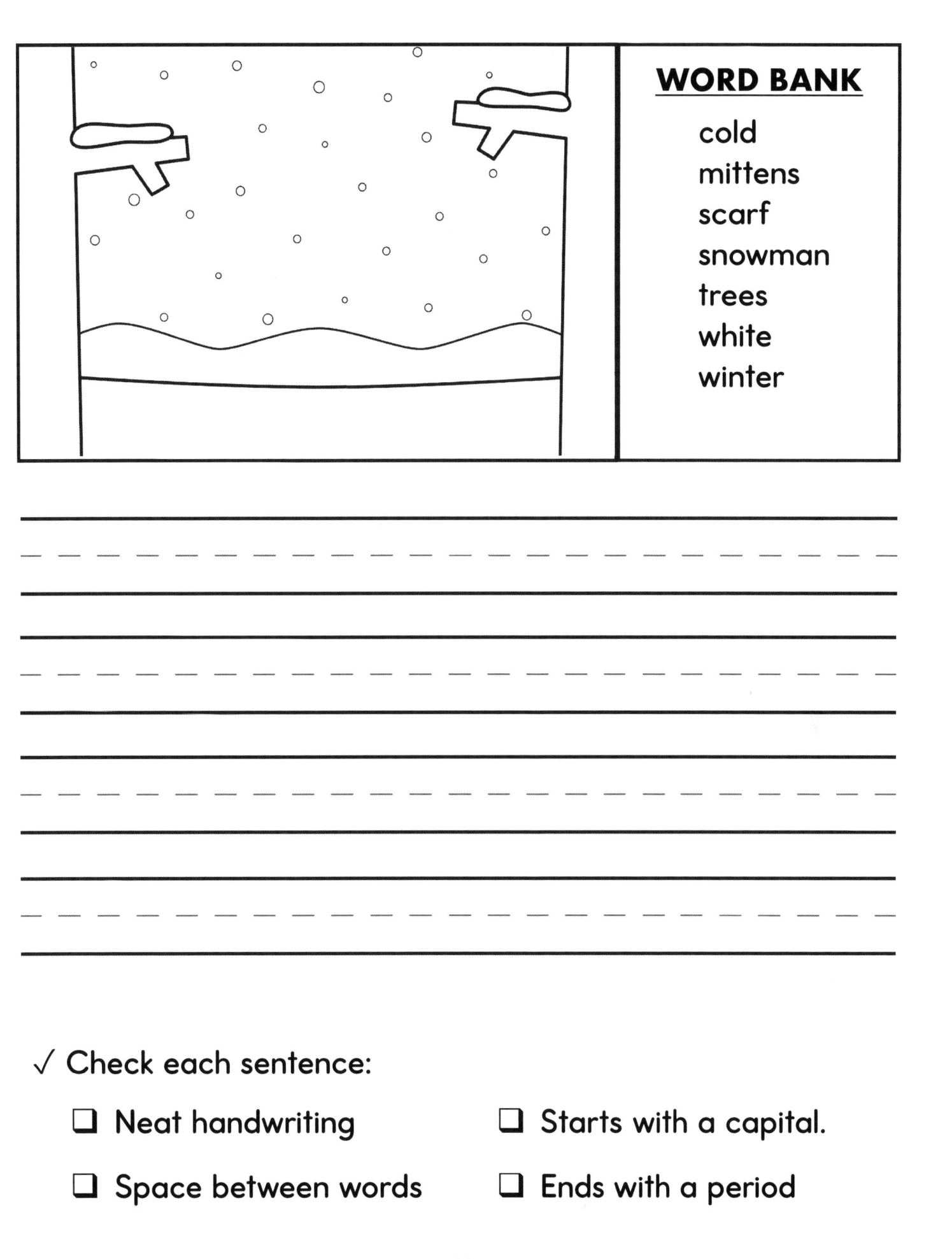

WORD BANK

cold
mittens
scarf
snowman
trees
white
winter

✓ Check each sentence:

❑ Neat handwriting ❑ Starts with a capital.

❑ Space between words ❑ Ends with a period

WORD BANK

grass
kids
outside
park
playground
sandbox
slide
swing

✓ Check each sentence:

❏ Neat handwriting ❏ Starts with a capital.

❏ Space between words ❏ Ends with a period

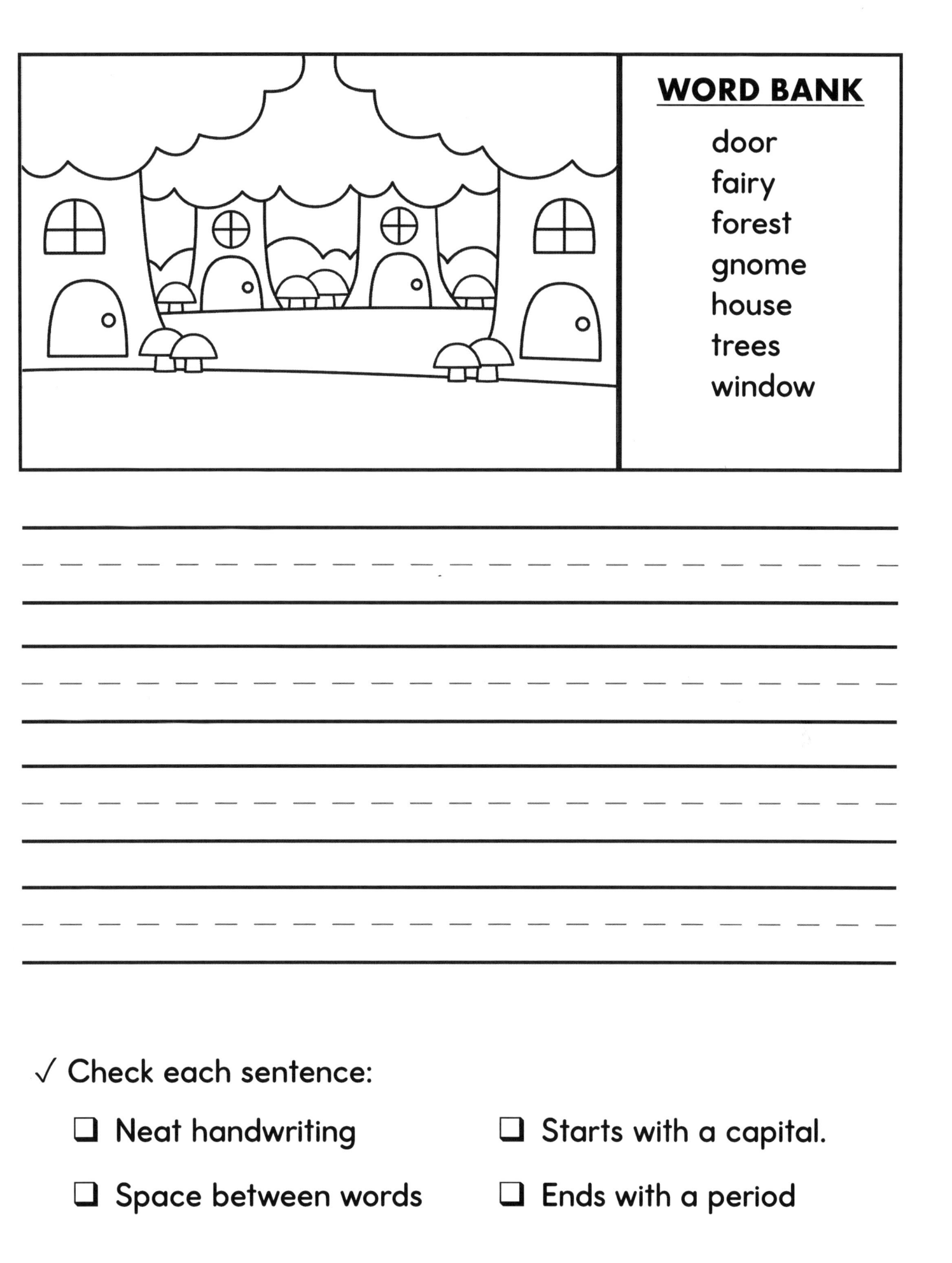

WORD BANK

door
fairy
forest
gnome
house
trees
window

✓ Check each sentence:

❑ Neat handwriting ❑ Starts with a capital.

❑ Space between words ❑ Ends with a period

WORD BANK

grass
hike
hill
mountains
nature
picnic

✓ Check each sentence:

❏ Neat handwriting ❏ Starts with a capital.

❏ Space between words ❏ Ends with a period

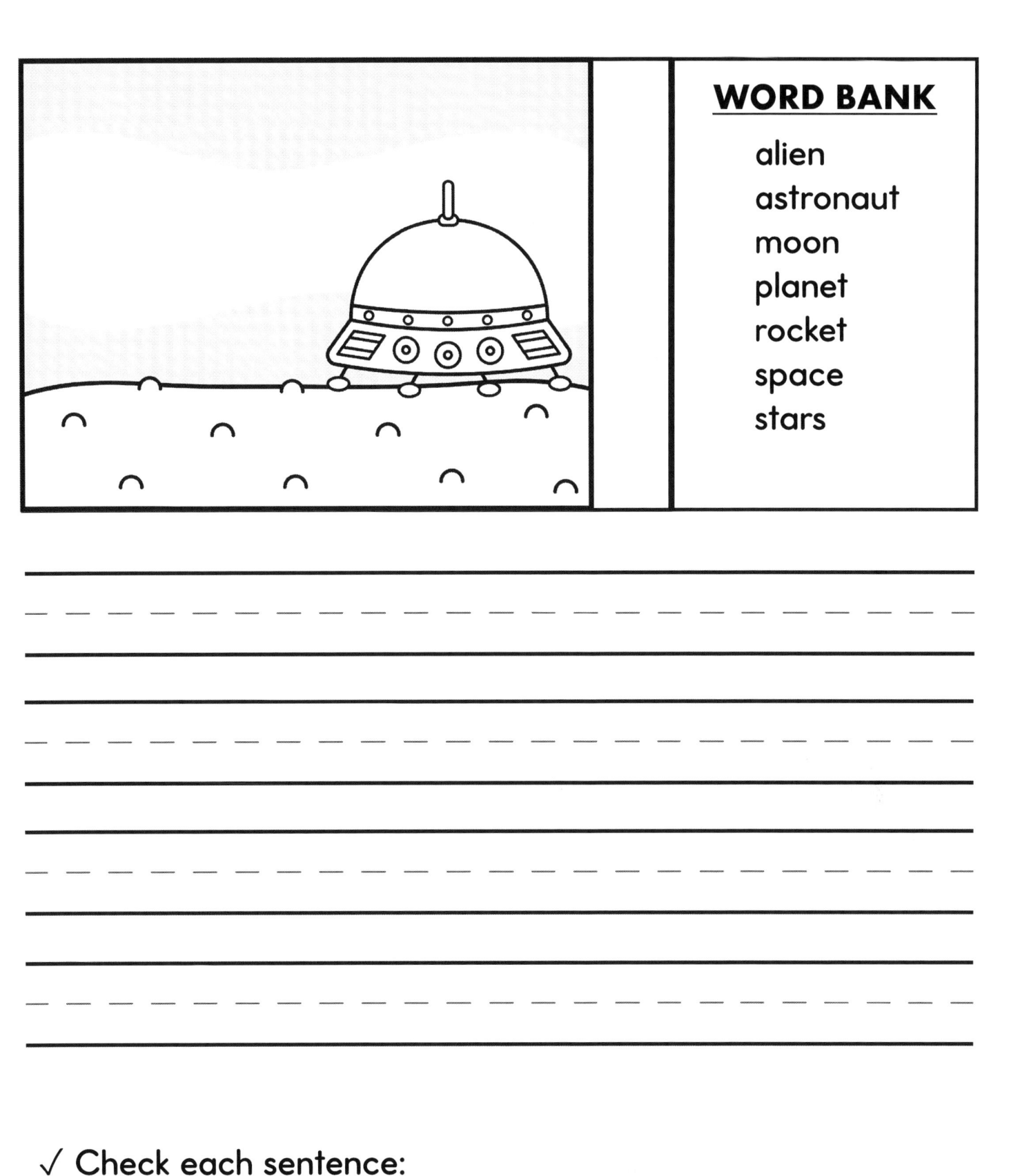

WORD BANK

alien
astronaut
moon
planet
rocket
space
stars

✓ Check each sentence:

❏ Neat handwriting ❏ Starts with a capital.

❏ Space between words ❏ Ends with a period

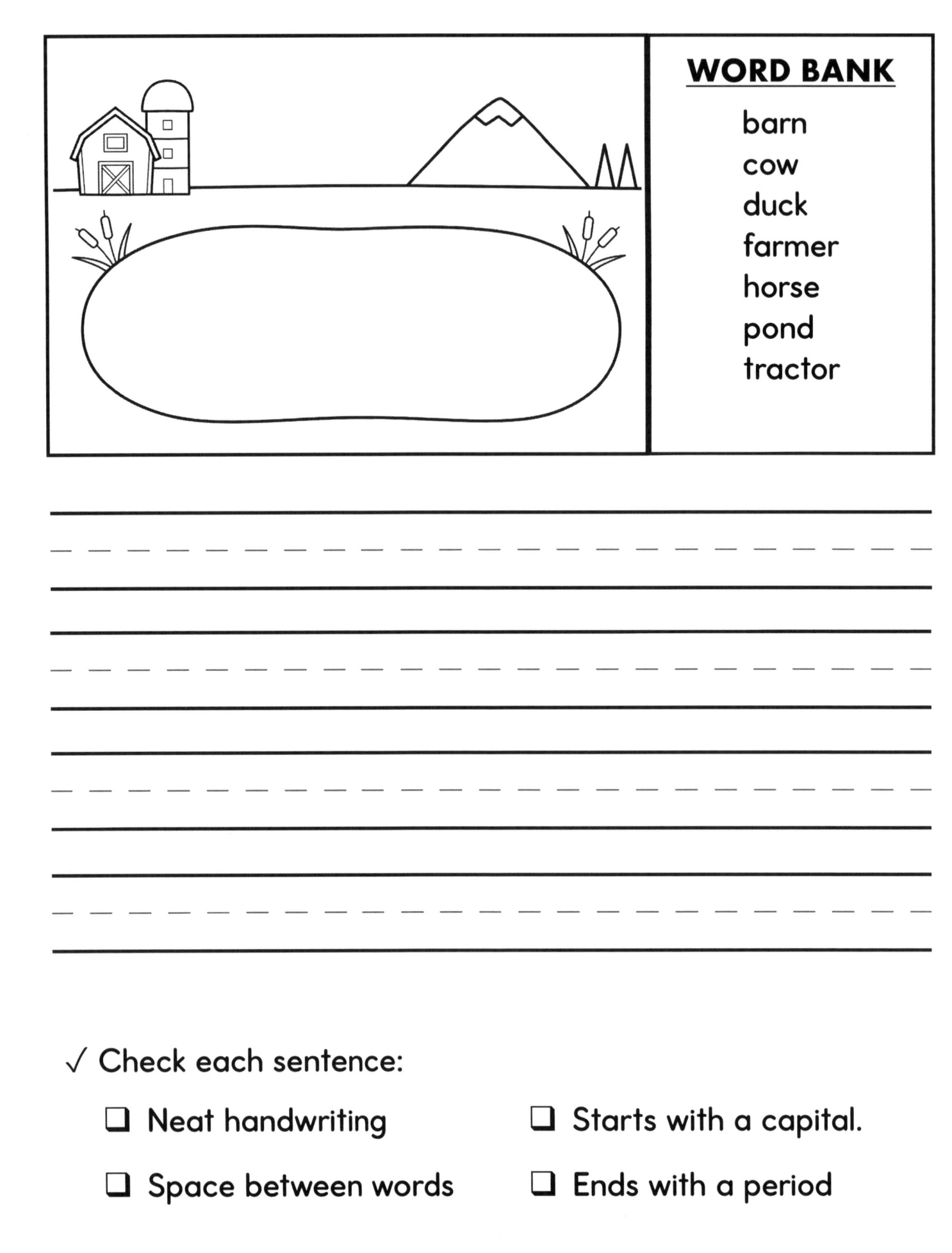

WORD BANK

barn
cow
duck
farmer
horse
pond
tractor

✓ Check each sentence:

❑ Neat handwriting ❑ Starts with a capital.

❑ Space between words ❑ Ends with a period

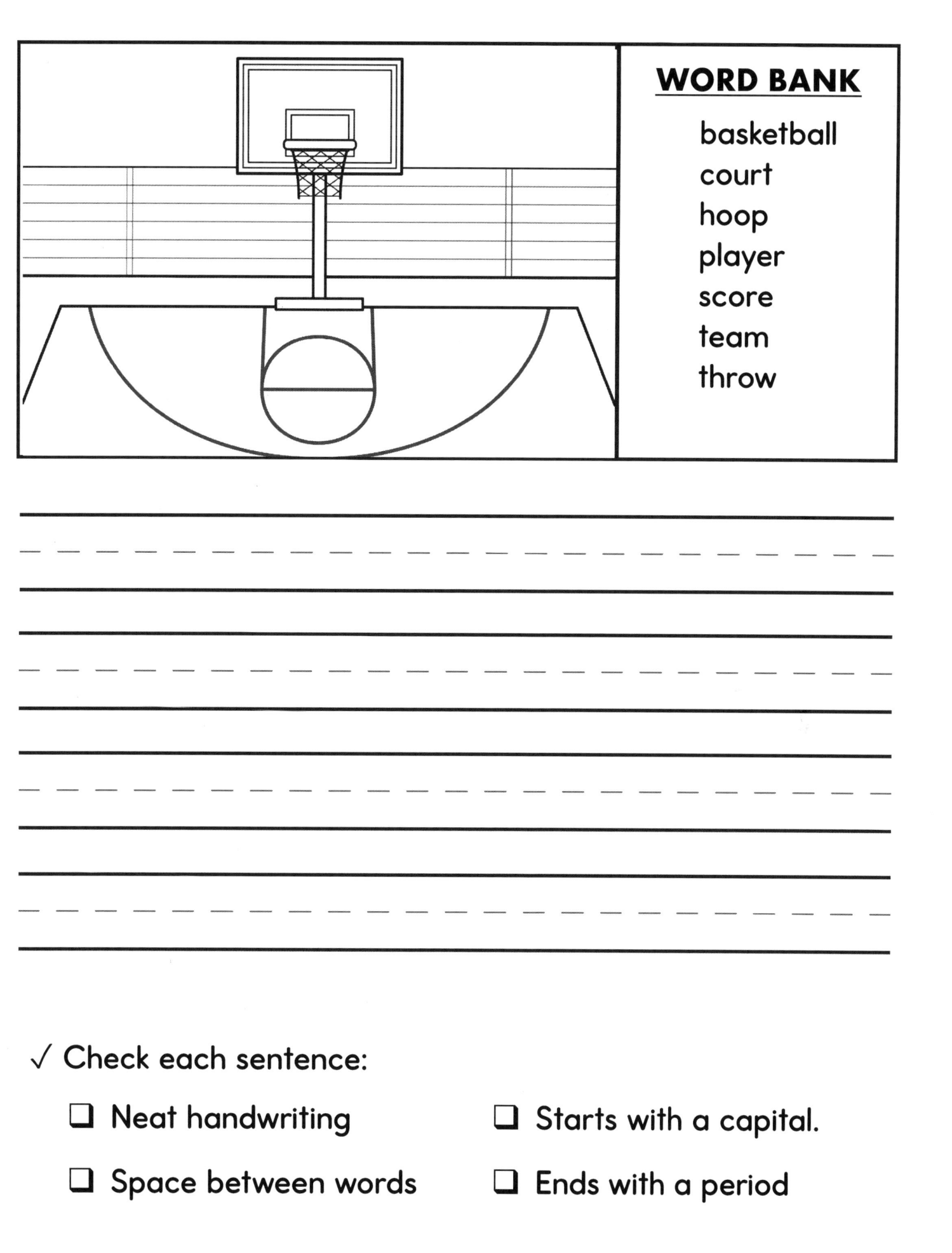

WORD BANK

basketball
court
hoop
player
score
team
throw

✓ Check each sentence:

❏ Neat handwriting ❏ Starts with a capital.

❏ Space between words ❏ Ends with a period

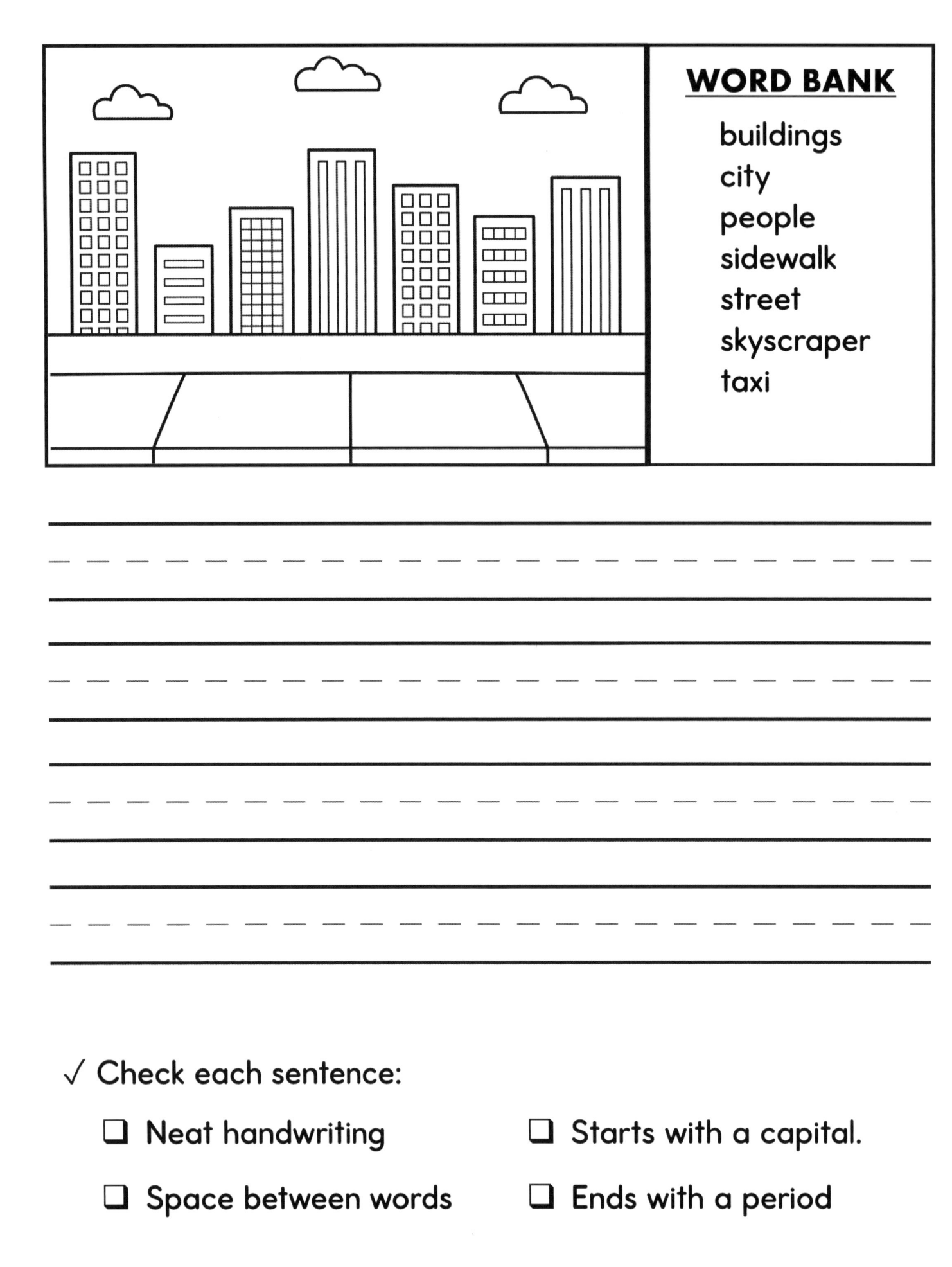

WORD BANK

buildings
city
people
sidewalk
street
skyscraper
taxi

_____

_____

_____

_____

✓ Check each sentence:

❑ Neat handwriting ❑ Starts with a capital.

❑ Space between words ❑ Ends with a period

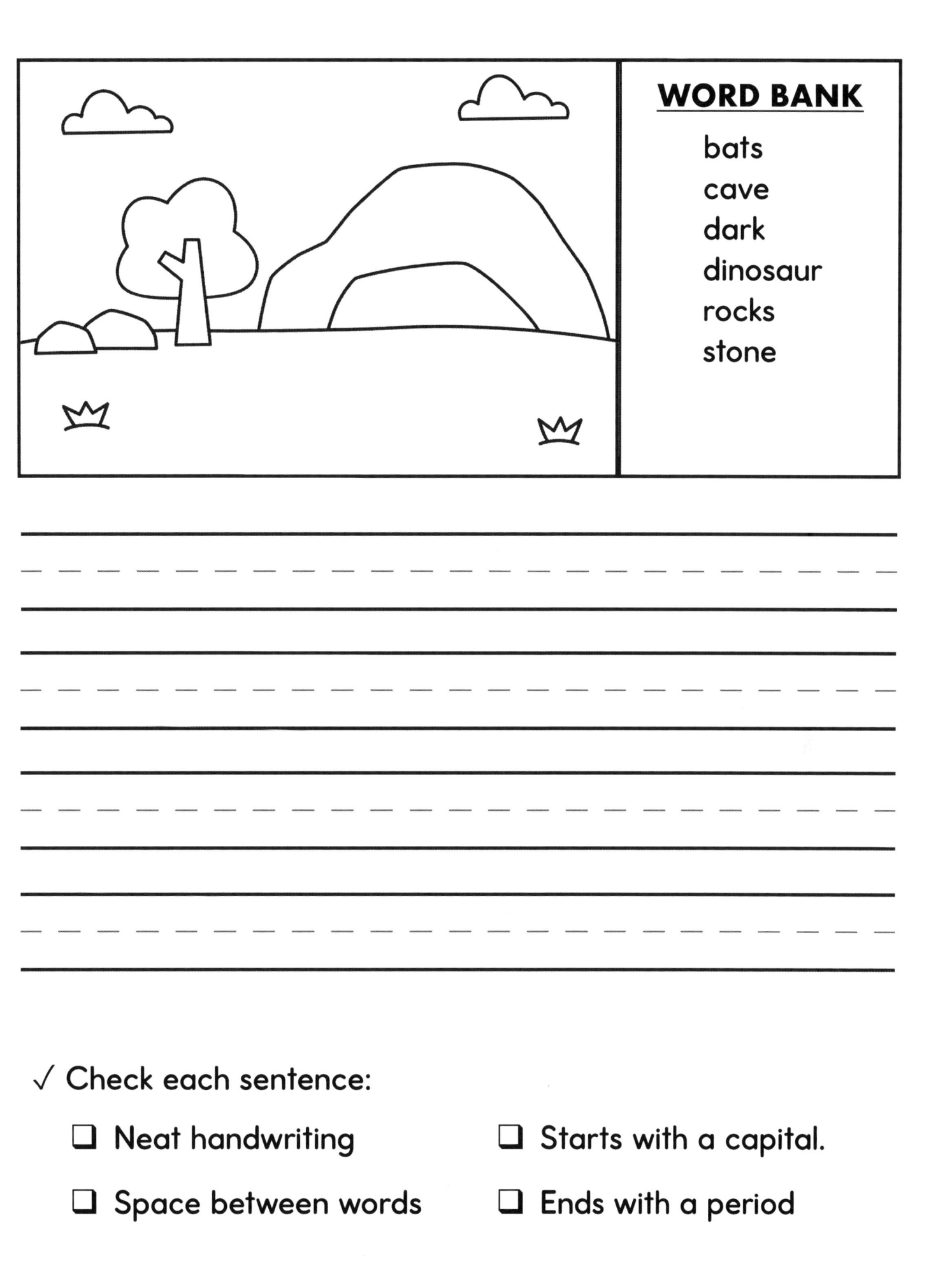

WORD BANK

bats
cave
dark
dinosaur
rocks
stone

✓ Check each sentence:

❏ Neat handwriting ❏ Starts with a capital.

❏ Space between words ❏ Ends with a period

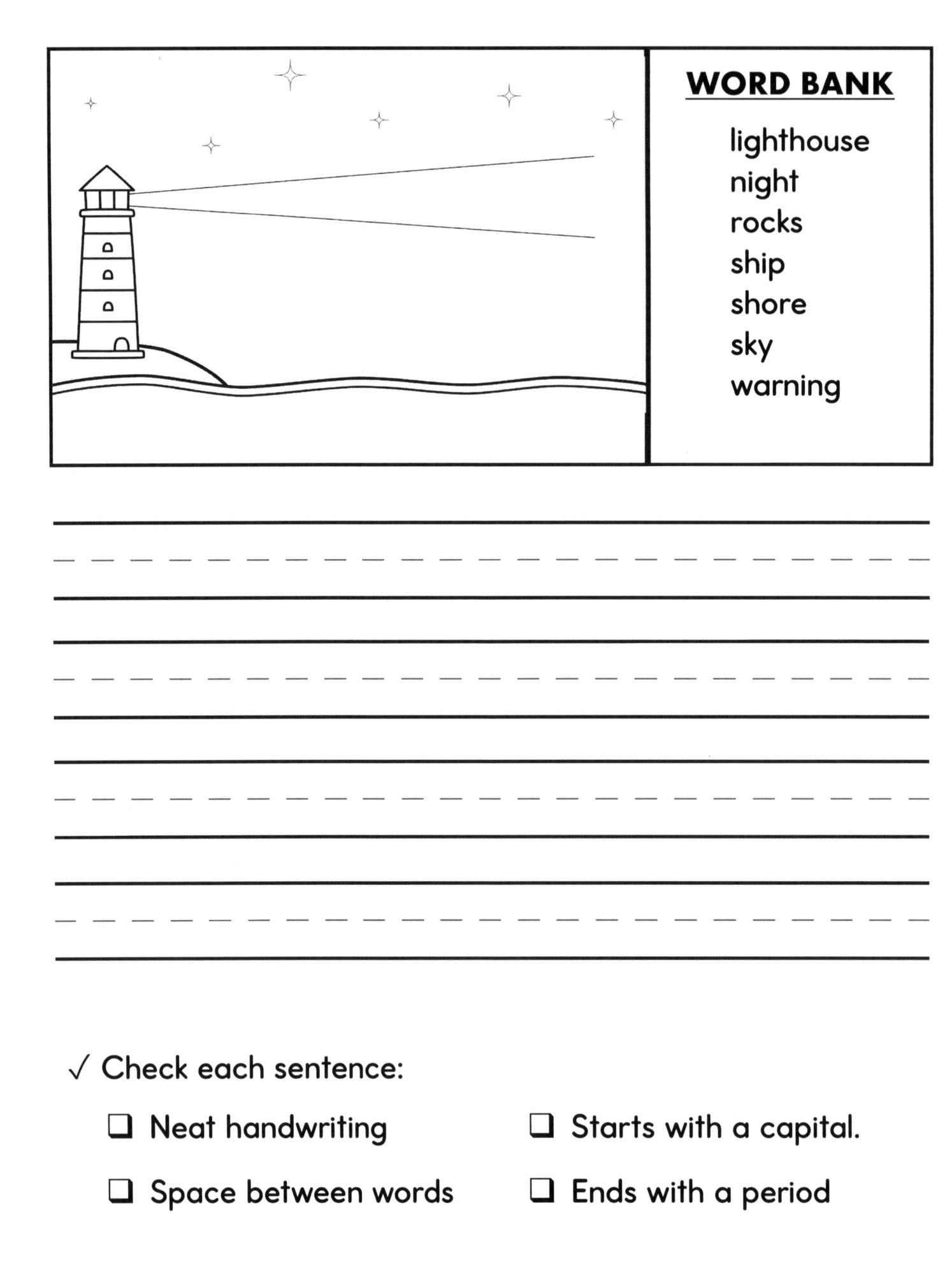

WORD BANK

lighthouse
night
rocks
ship
shore
sky
warning

✓ Check each sentence:

❑ Neat handwriting ❑ Starts with a capital.

❑ Space between words ❑ Ends with a period

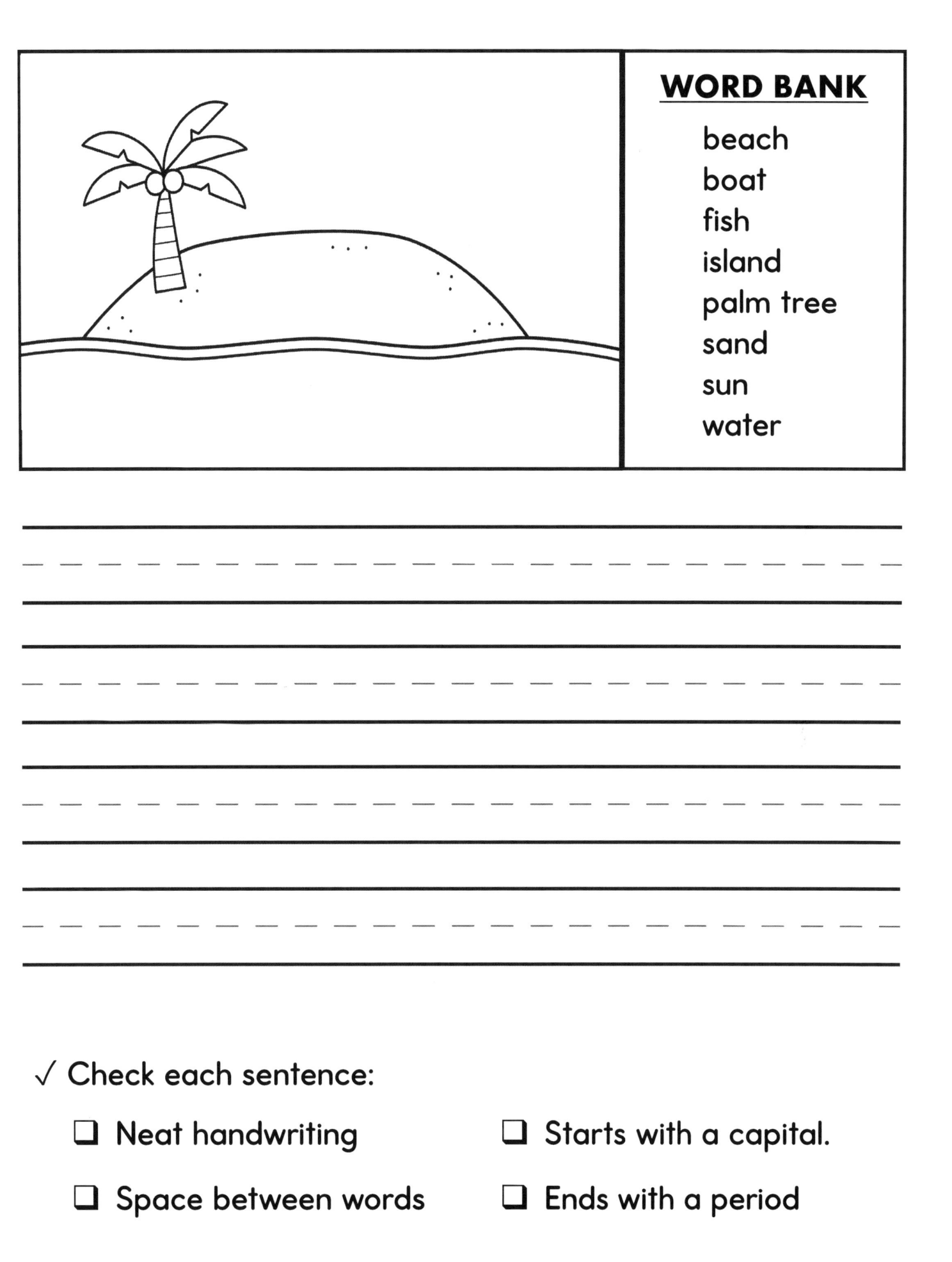

WORD BANK

beach
boat
fish
island
palm tree
sand
sun
water

✓ Check each sentence:

❏ Neat handwriting   ❏ Starts with a capital.

❏ Space between words   ❏ Ends with a period

WORD BANK

coaster
fair
fast
fun
high
ride
ticket

✓ Check each sentence:

❏ Neat handwriting ❏ Starts with a capital.

❏ Space between words ❏ Ends with a period

WORD BANK

door
family
fence
garage
house
neighbor
windows
yard

✓ Check each sentence:

❑ Neat handwriting ❑ Starts with a capital.

❑ Space between words ❑ Ends with a period

WORD BANK

birds
jungle
monkey
plants
swing
tree
vines

✓ Check each sentence:

❑ Neat handwriting   ❑ Starts with a capital.

❑ Space between words   ❑ Ends with a period

WORD BANK

autumn
fall
ground
leaves
rake
pile
tree
wind

✓ Check each sentence:

❏ Neat handwriting   ❏ Starts with a capital.

❏ Space between words   ❏ Ends with a period

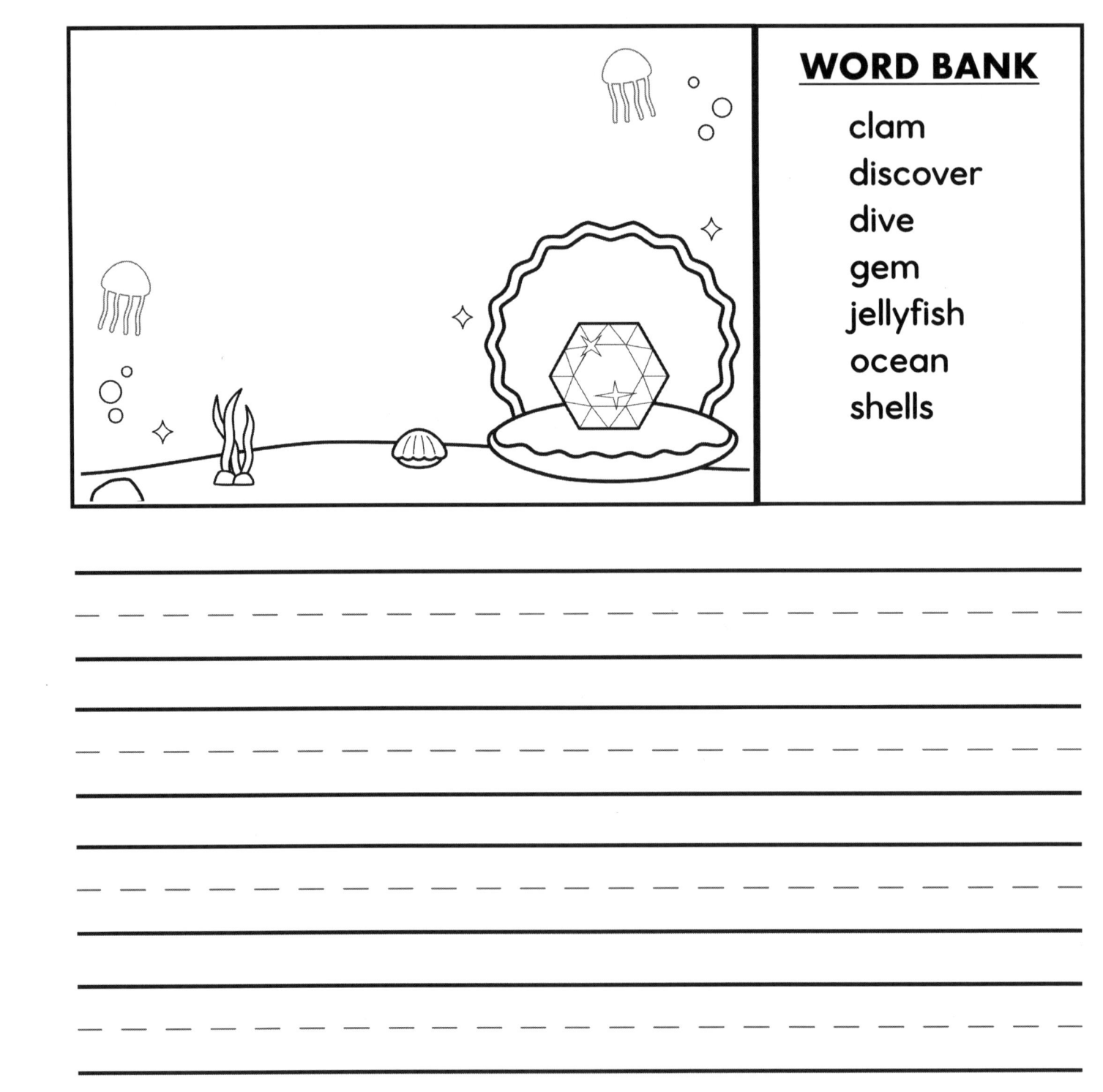

WORD BANK

clam
discover
dive
gem
jellyfish
ocean
shells

✓ Check each sentence:

❑ Neat handwriting   ❑ Starts with a capital.

❑ Space between words   ❑ Ends with a period

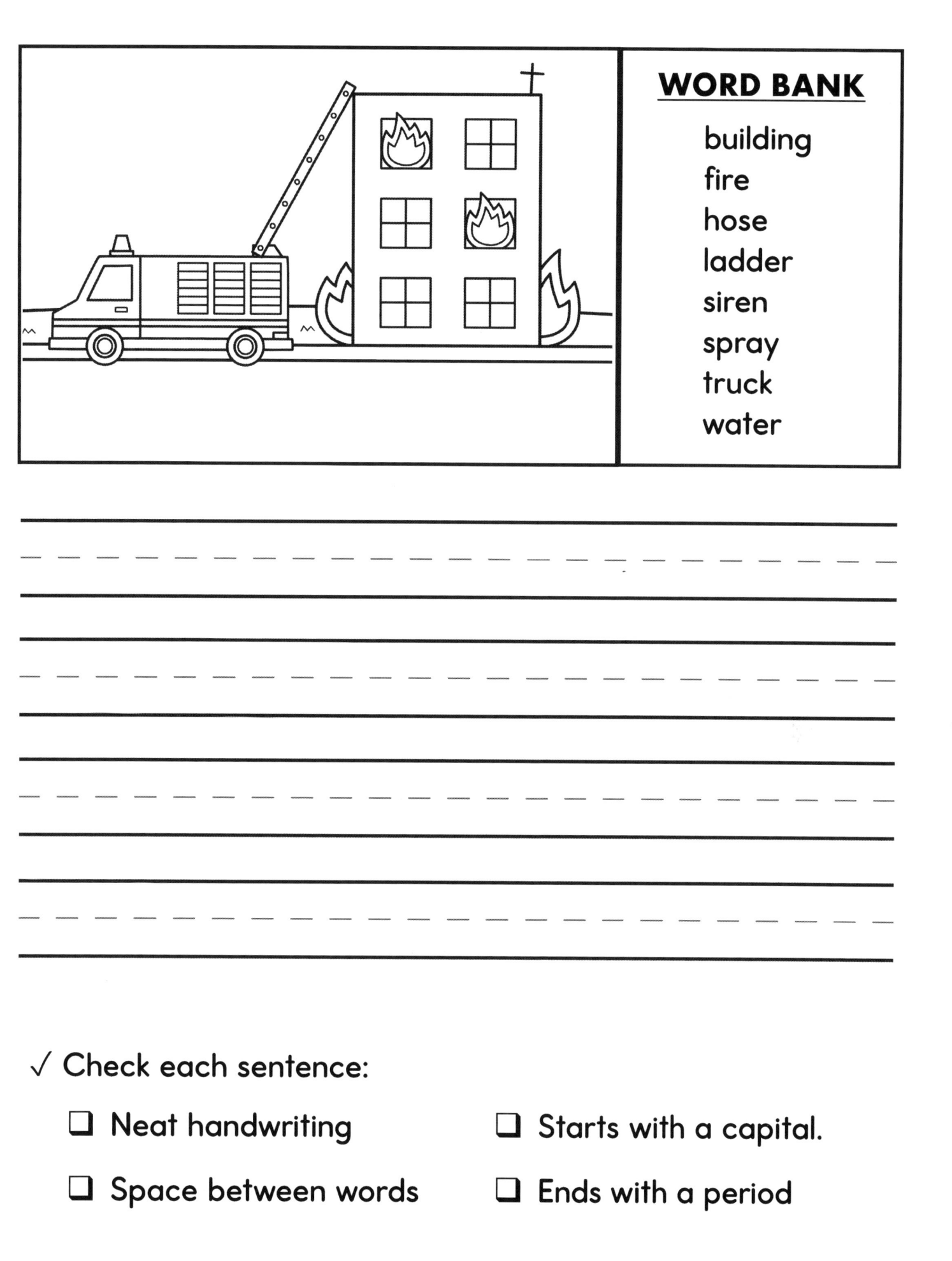

WORD BANK

building
fire
hose
ladder
siren
spray
truck
water

✓ Check each sentence:

❏ Neat handwriting ❏ Starts with a capital.

❏ Space between words ❏ Ends with a period

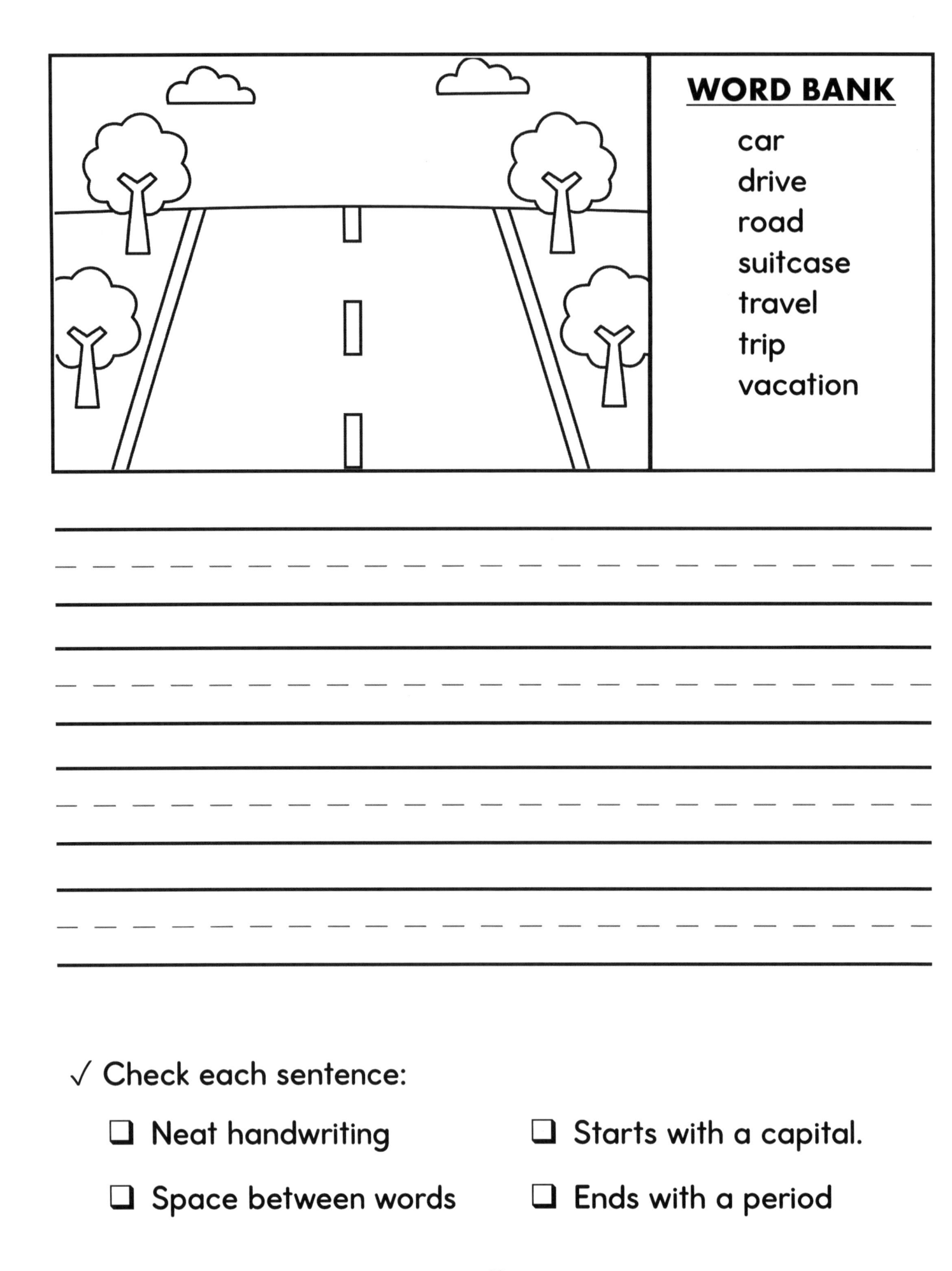

WORD BANK

car
drive
road
suitcase
travel
trip
vacation

✓ Check each sentence:

❑ Neat handwriting ❑ Starts with a capital.

❑ Space between words ❑ Ends with a period

WORD BANK

candy
frosting
gingerbread
gumdrops
licorice
house
lollipop
taste

✓ Check each sentence:

❑ Neat handwriting   ❑ Starts with a capital.

❑ Space between words   ❑ Ends with a period

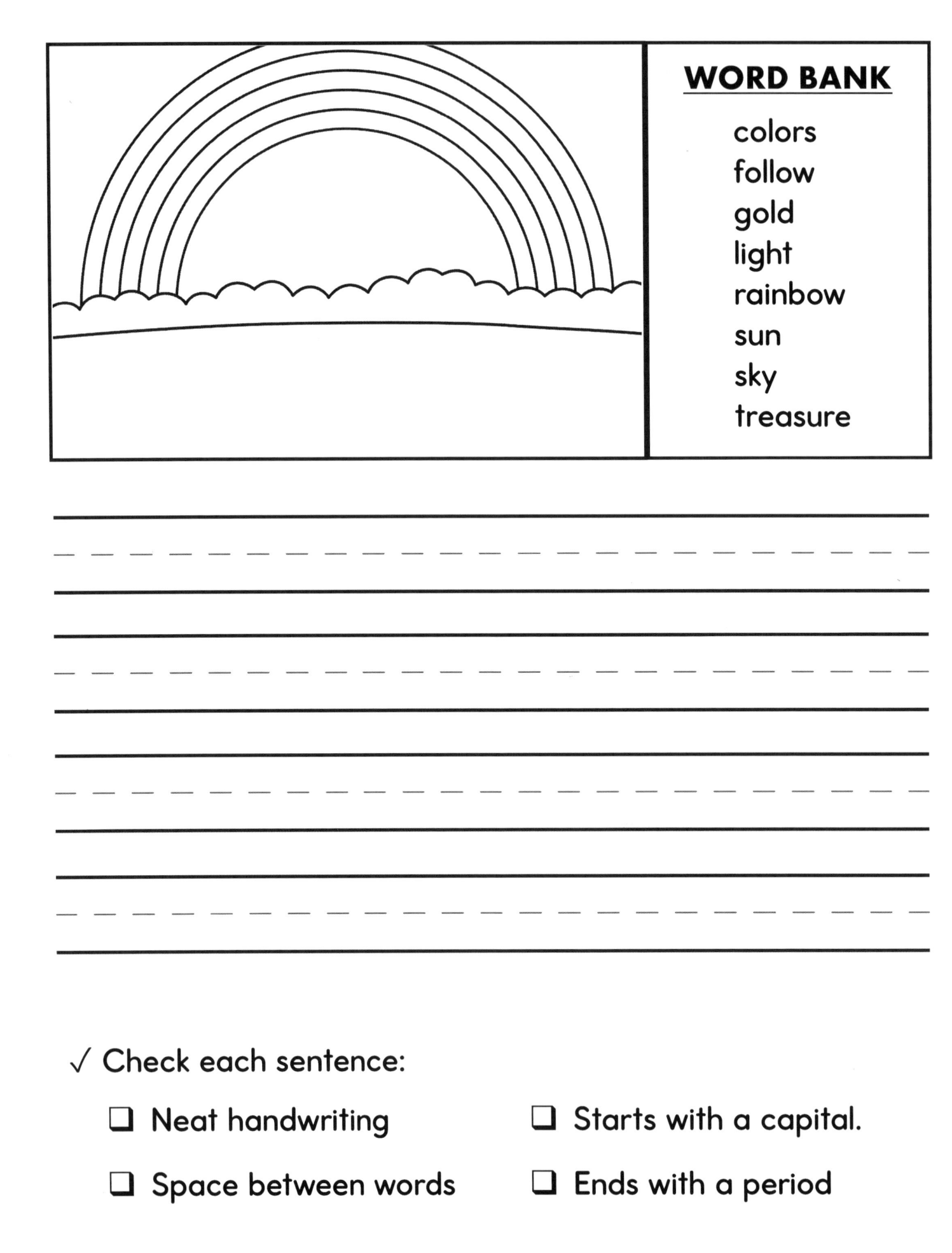

WORD BANK

colors
follow
gold
light
rainbow
sun
sky
treasure

✓ Check each sentence:

❑ Neat handwriting ❑ Starts with a capital.

❑ Space between words ❑ Ends with a period

WORD BANK

branch
butterfly
caterpillar
cocoon
crawl
leaf
spring
wings

✓ Check each sentence:

❑ Neat handwriting ❑ Starts with a capital.

❑ Space between words ❑ Ends with a period

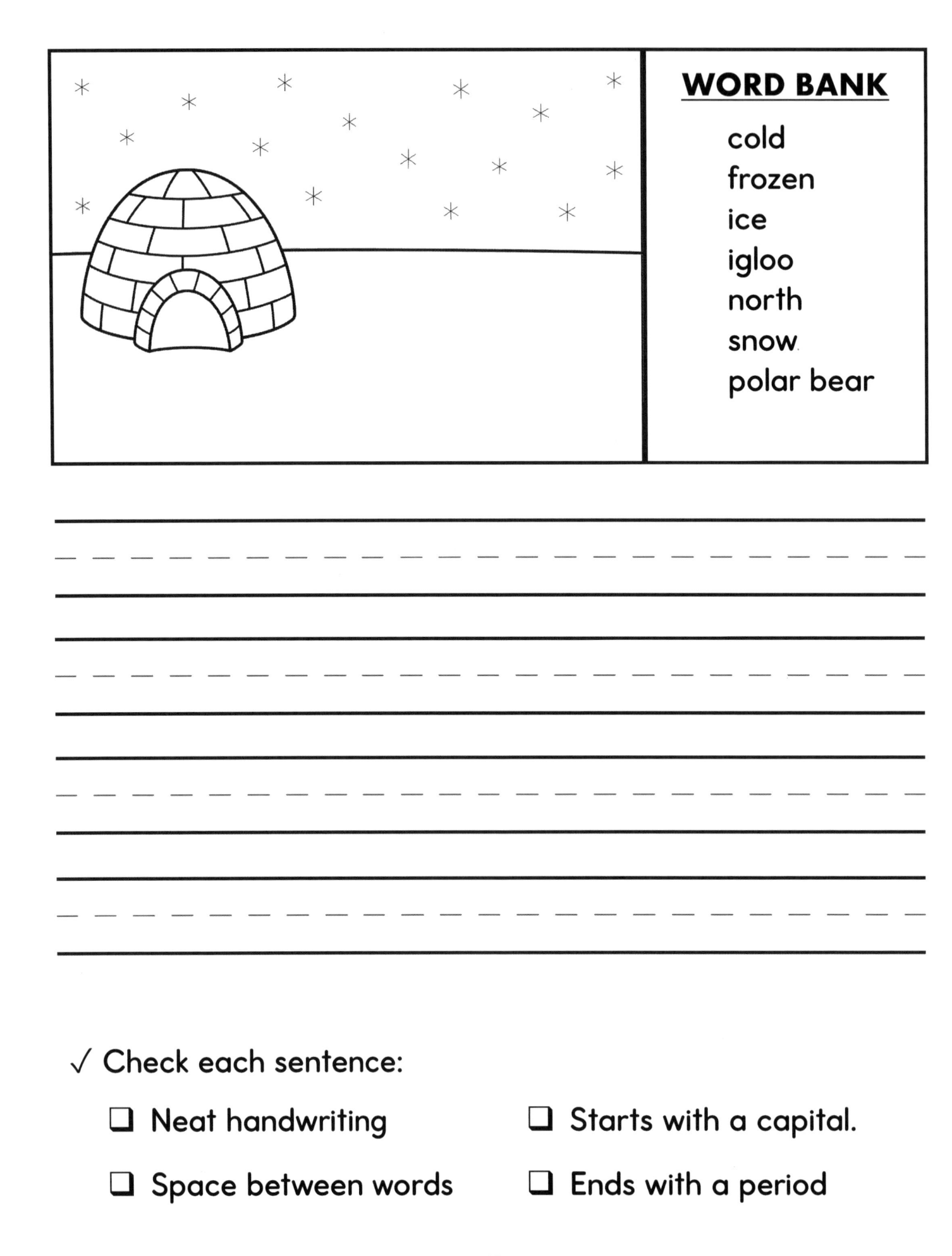

WORD BANK

cold
frozen
ice
igloo
north
snow
polar bear

✓ Check each sentence:

❑ Neat handwriting ❑ Starts with a capital.

❑ Space between words ❑ Ends with a period

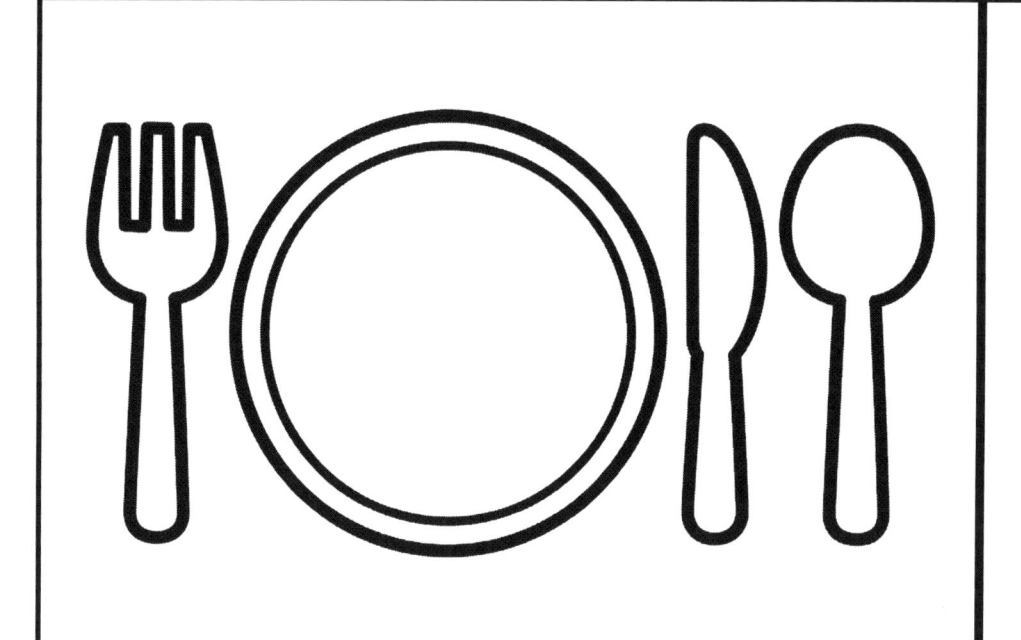

WORD BANK

eat
food
fork
knife
lunch
plate
spoon
taste

✓ Check each sentence:

❏ Neat handwriting ❏ Starts with a capital.

❏ Space between words ❏ Ends with a period

WORD BANK

bed
night
room
sleep
toys
window

✓ Check each sentence:

❑ Neat handwriting ❑ Starts with a capital.

❑ Space between words ❑ Ends with a period

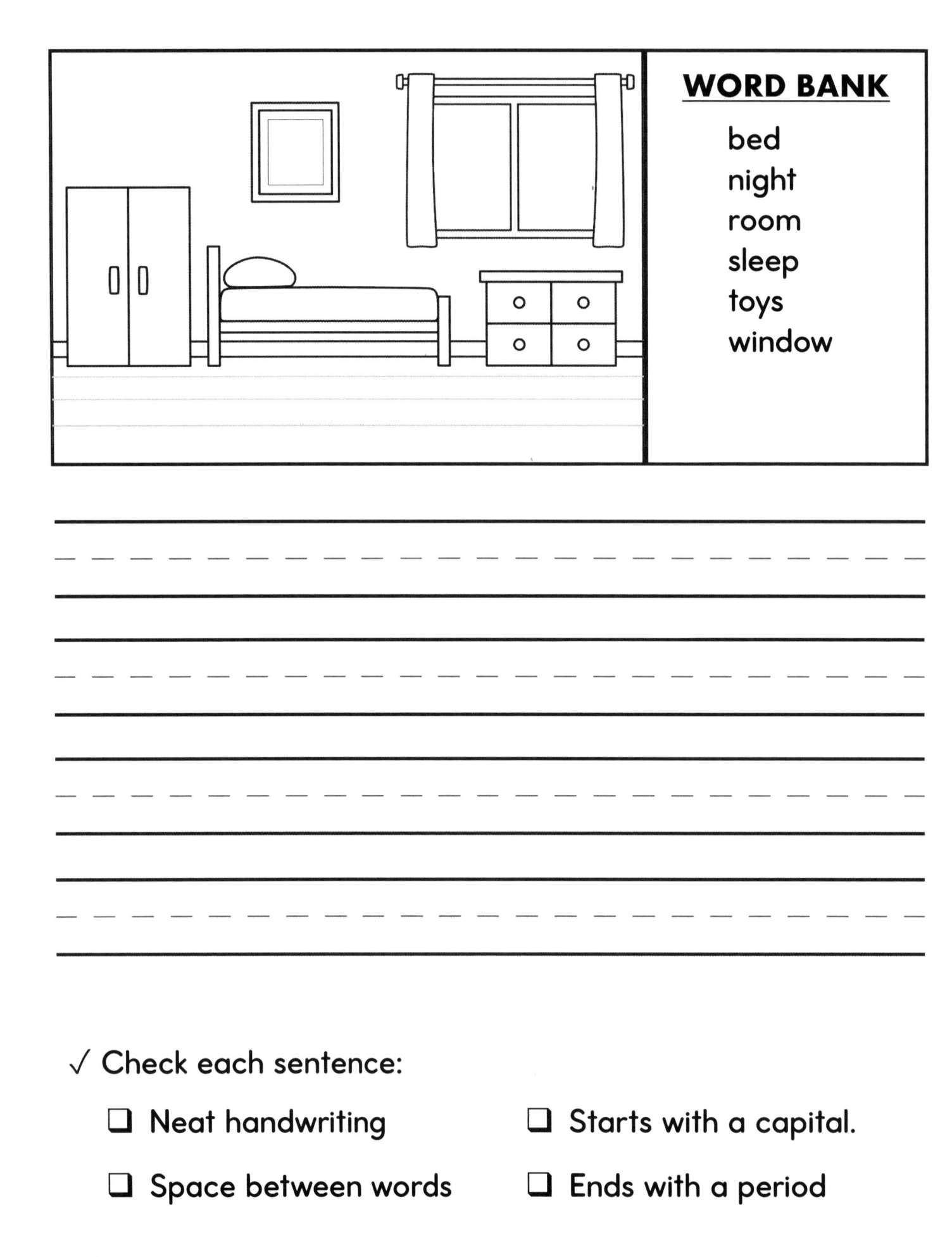

WORD BANK

chest
gold
ocean
pirate
sea
ship
treasure

✓ Check each sentence:

❏ Neat handwriting ❏ Starts with a capital.

❏ Space between words ❏ Ends with a period

WORD BANK

cars
crash
engine
fast
finish line
flag
race

✓ Check each sentence:

❑ Neat handwriting

❑ Space between words

❑ Starts with a capital.

❑ Ends with a period

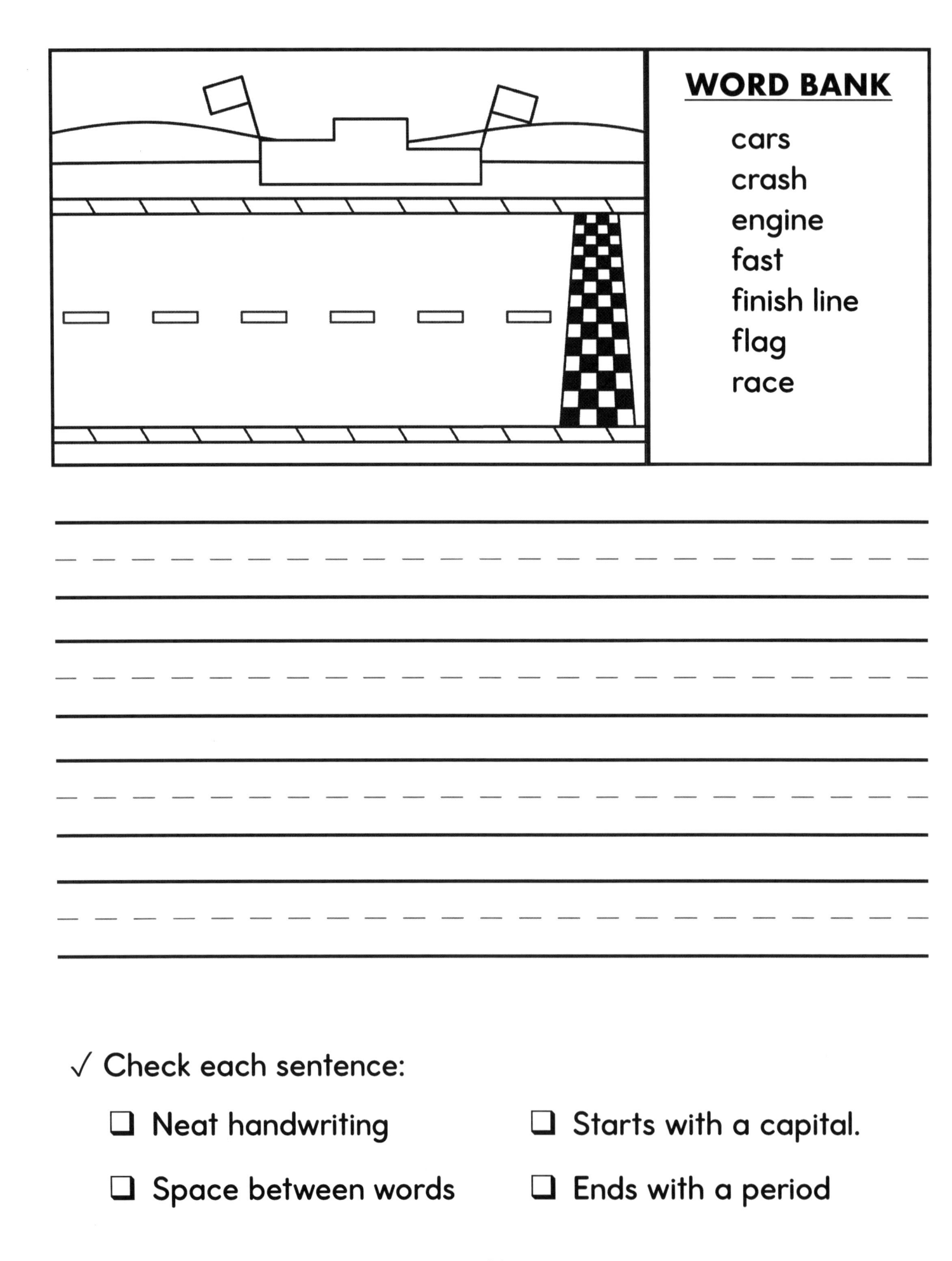

WORD BANK

cloud
rain
storm
spin
tornado
weather
wind

✓ Check each sentence:

❑ Neat handwriting ❑ Starts with a capital.

❑ Space between words ❑ Ends with a period

WORD BANK

erupt
fire
heat
lava
melt
mountain
volcano

✓ Check each sentence:

❑ Neat handwriting   ❑ Starts with a capital.

❑ Space between words   ❑ Ends with a period

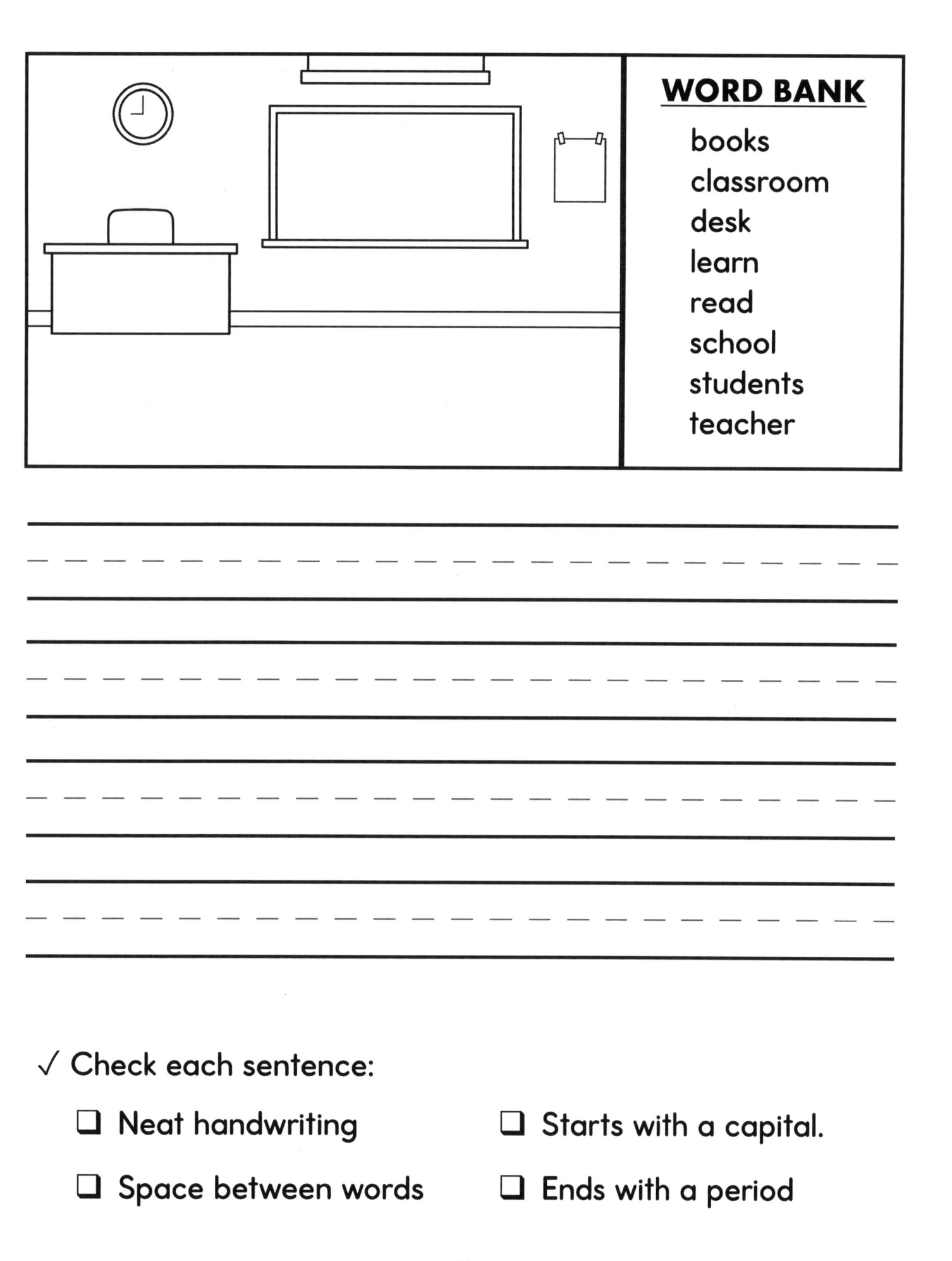

WORD BANK

books
classroom
desk
learn
read
school
students
teacher

✓ Check each sentence:

❑ Neat handwriting   ❑ Starts with a capital.

❑ Space between words   ❑ Ends with a period

WORD BANK

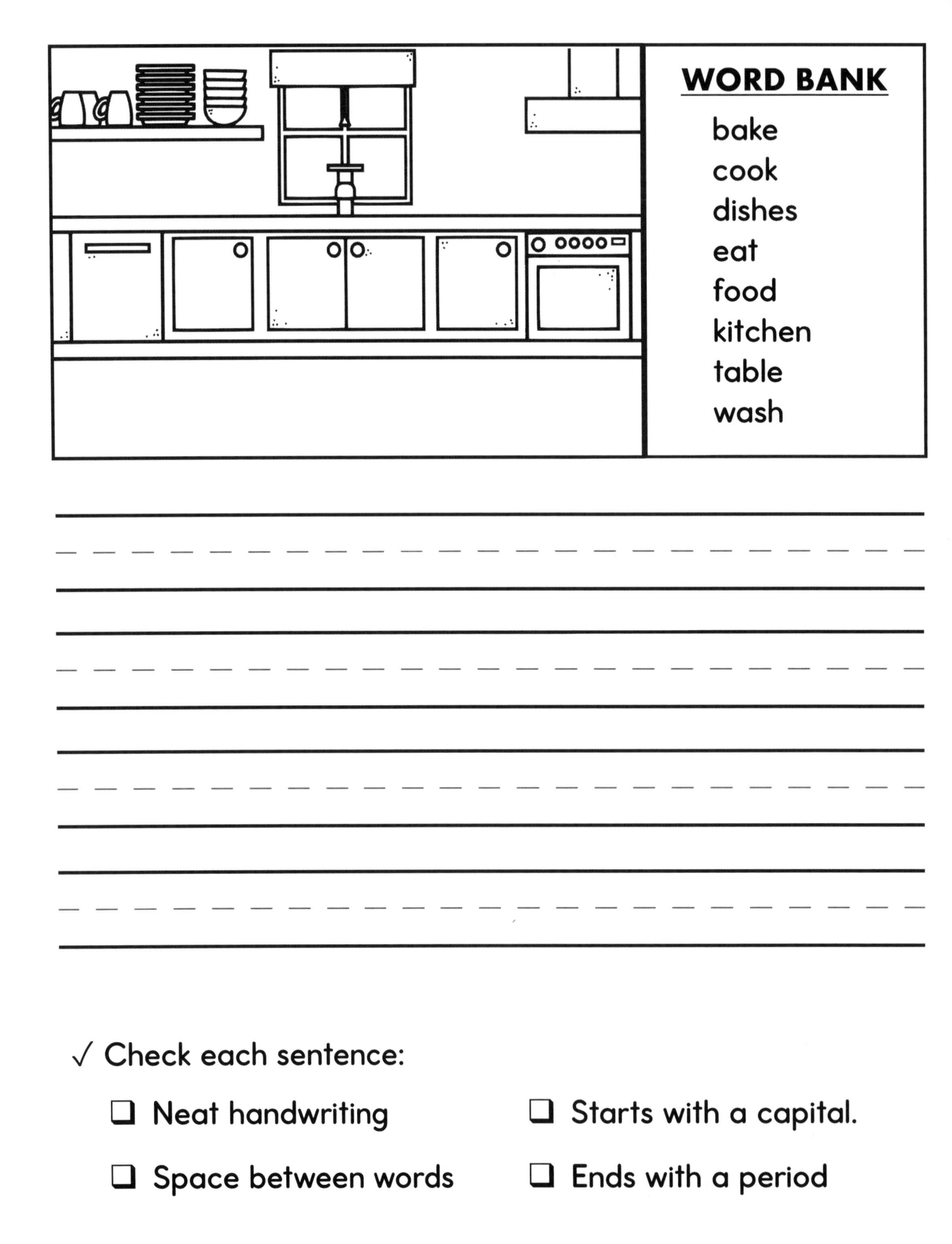

bake
cook
dishes
eat
food
kitchen
table
wash

✓ Check each sentence:

❑ Neat handwriting   ❑ Starts with a capital.

❑ Space between words   ❑ Ends with a period

WORD BANK
band
audience
clap
curtain
music
show
sing
stage

✓ Check each sentence:

❑ Neat handwriting

❑ Space between words

❑ Starts with a capital.

❑ Ends with a period

WORD BANK

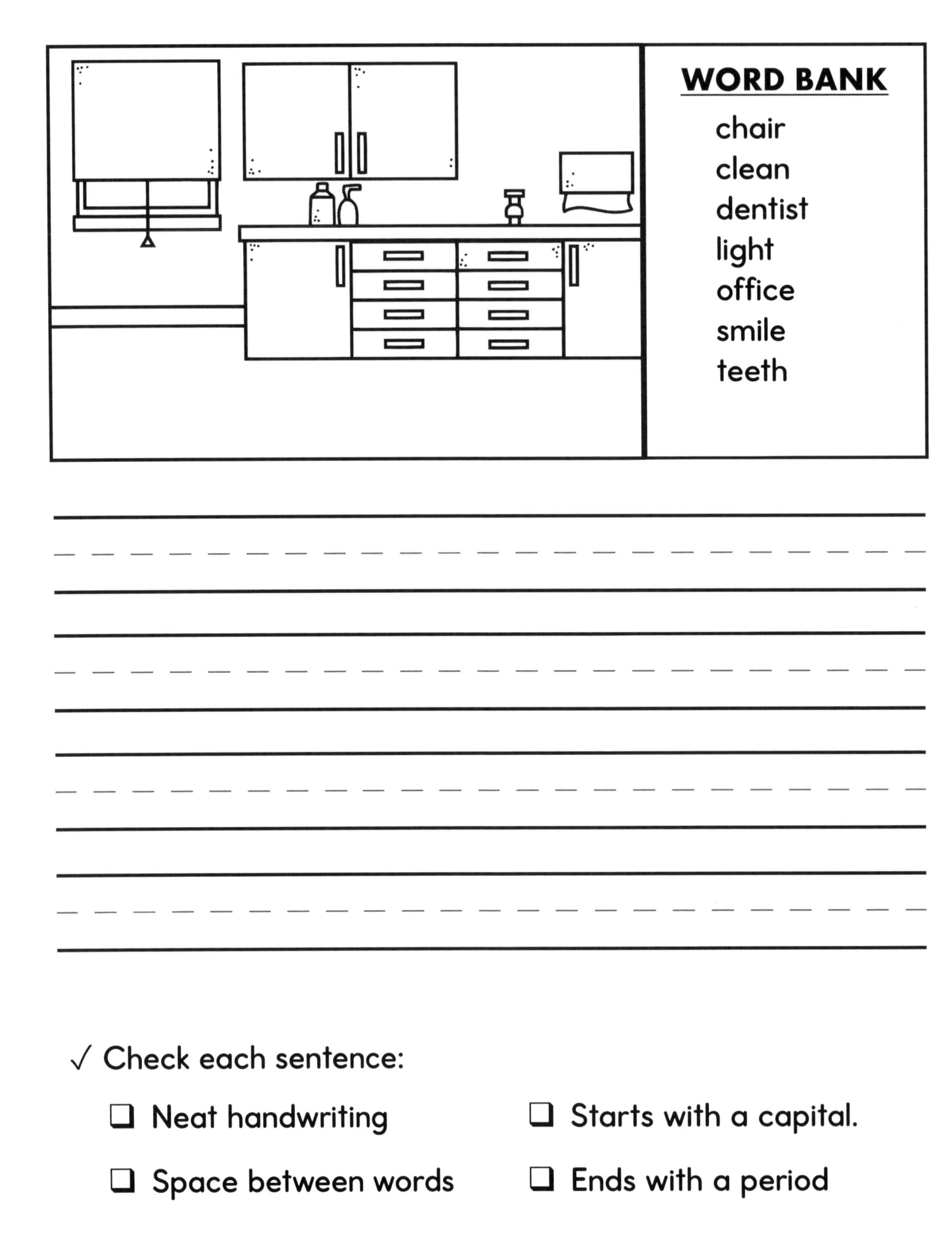

chair
clean
dentist
light
office
smile
teeth

✓ Check each sentence:

❑ Neat handwriting

❑ Space between words

❑ Starts with a capital.

❑ Ends with a period

WORD BANK

chimney
Christmas
eve
reindeer
roof
Santa
sleigh
sky

✓ Check each sentence:

❏ Neat handwriting   ❏ Starts with a capital.

❏ Space between words   ❏ Ends with a period

WORD BANK

art
exhibit
fossils
history
learn
museum
touch
tour

✓ Check each sentence:

❏ Neat handwriting　　❏ Starts with a capital.

❏ Space between words　　❏ Ends with a period

WORD BANK

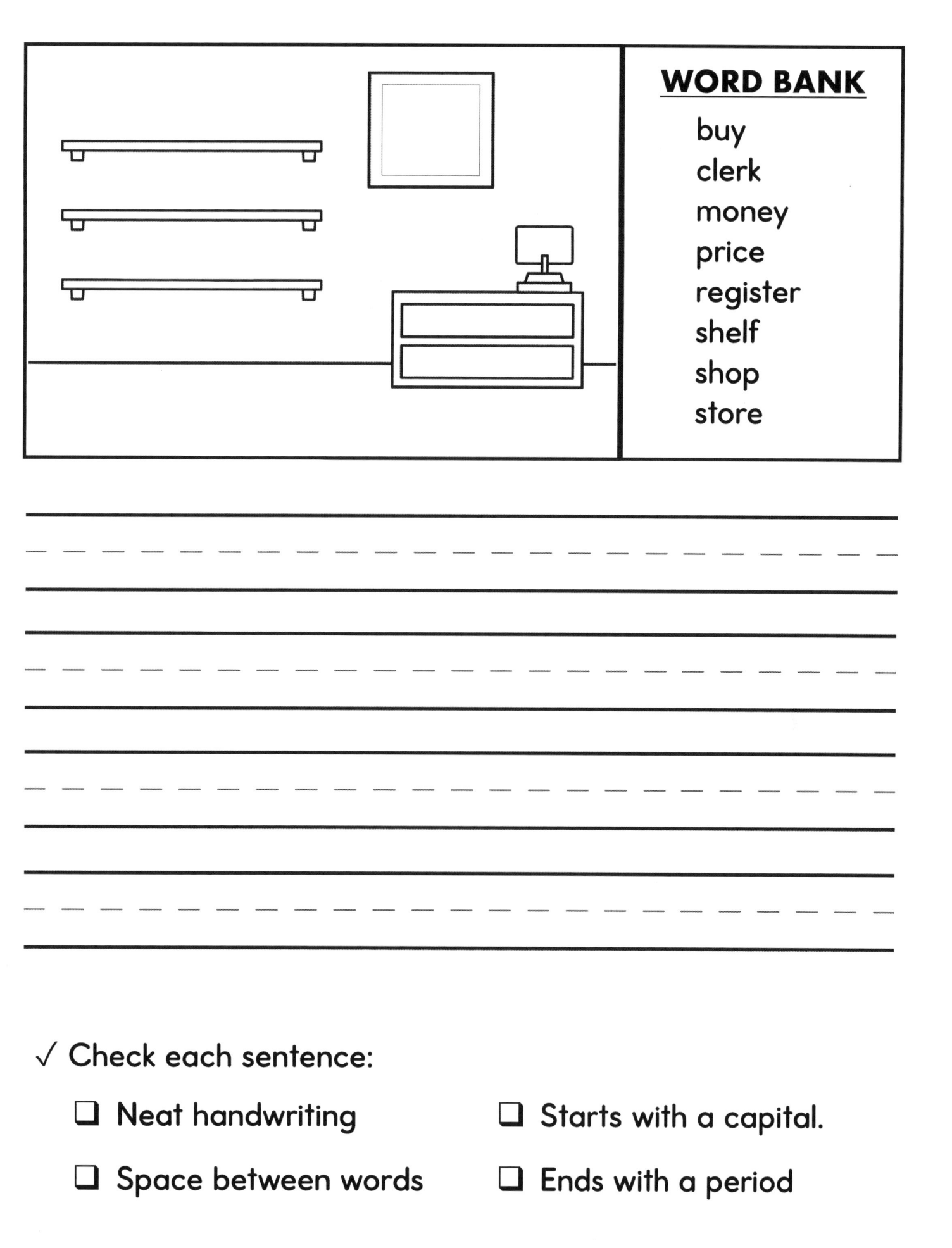

buy
clerk
money
price
register
shelf
shop
store

✓ Check each sentence:

- ❏ Neat handwriting
- ❏ Space between words
- ❏ Starts with a capital.
- ❏ Ends with a period

WORD BANK
bike
friends
play
outdoors
summer
sunny

✓ Check each sentence:

❏ Neat handwriting ❏ Starts with a capital.

❏ Space between words ❏ Ends with a period

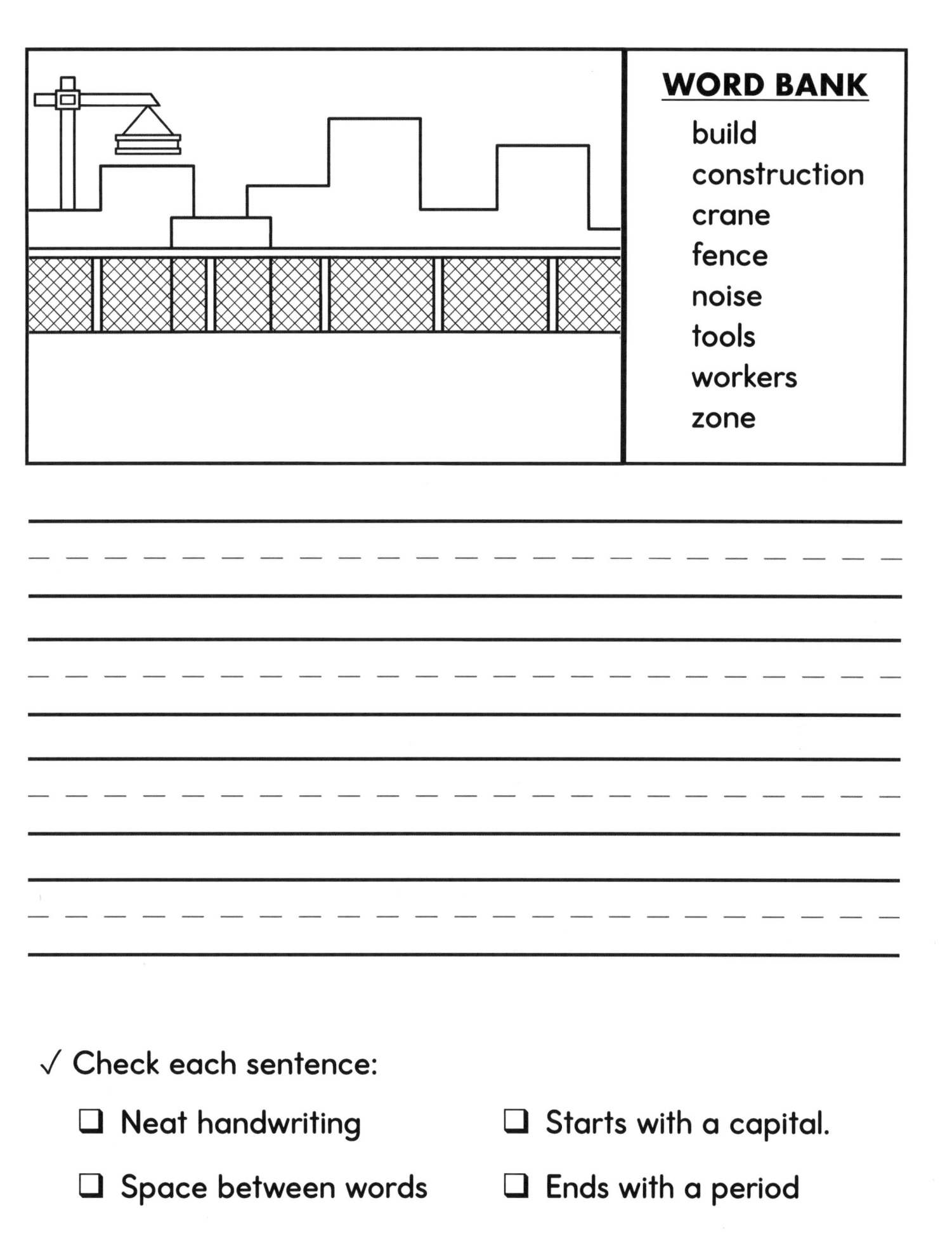

WORD BANK
build
construction
crane
fence
noise
tools
workers
zone

✓ Check each sentence:

❏ Neat handwriting ❏ Starts with a capital.

❏ Space between words ❏ Ends with a period

WORD BANK

castle
clouds
dragon
king
magic
queen
sky

✓ Check each sentence:

❏ Neat handwriting ❏ Starts with a capital.

❏ Space between words ❏ Ends with a period

WORD BANK

ballroom
dance
fancy
floor
lights
music

✓ Check each sentence:

❏ Neat handwriting ❏ Starts with a capital.

❏ Space between words ❏ Ends with a period

WORD BANK
bat
costume
Halloween
haunted
moon
night
spooky
witch

✓ Check each sentence:

❑ Neat handwriting   ❑ Starts with a capital.

❑ Space between words ❑ Ends with a period

WORD BANK

cloud
lightning
puddle
rain
sky
thunder
umbrella
wet

✓ Check each sentence:

❑ Neat handwriting   ❑ Starts with a capital.

❑ Space between words   ❑ Ends with a period

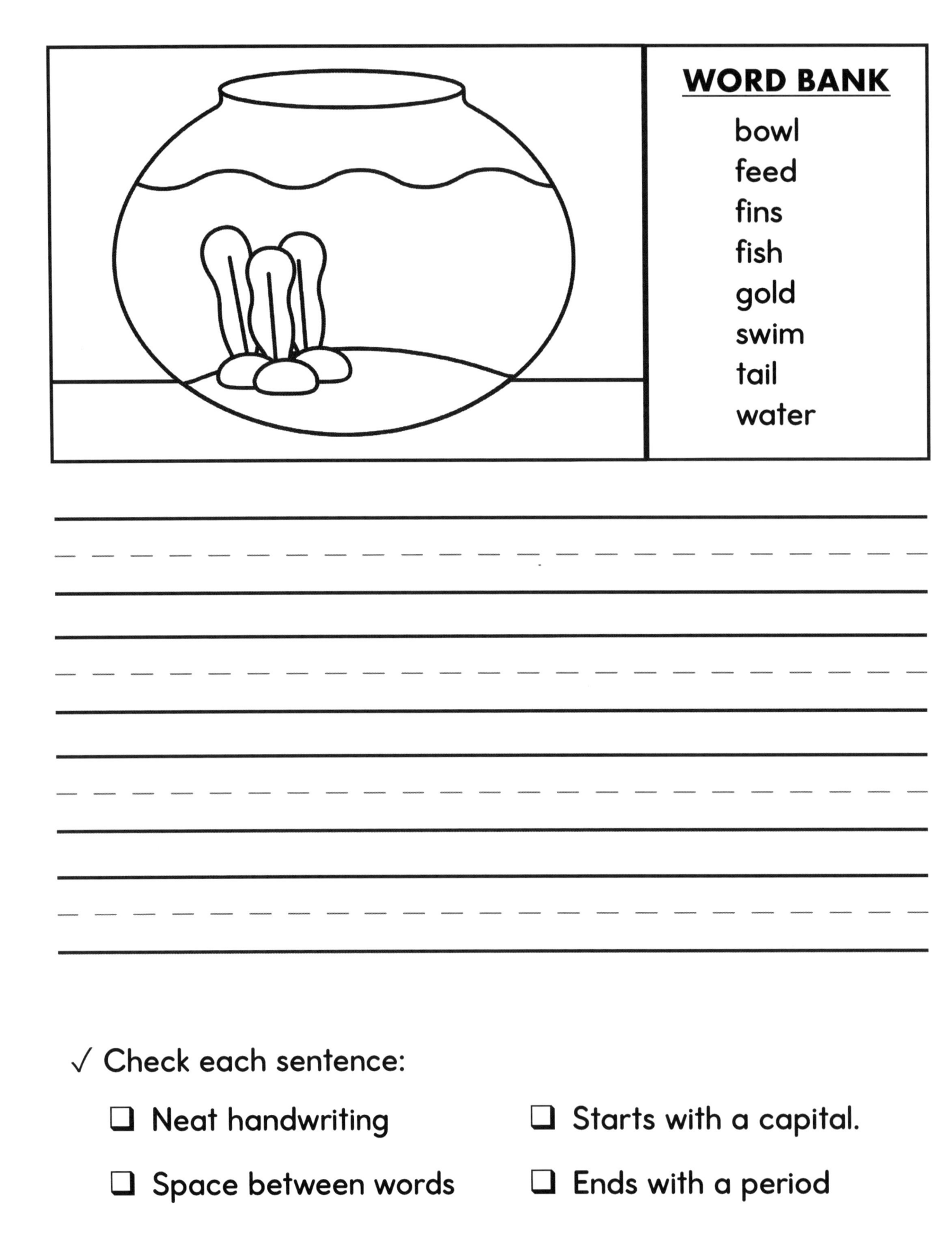

WORD BANK

bowl
feed
fins
fish
gold
swim
tail
water

✓ Check each sentence:

❑ Neat handwriting   ❑ Starts with a capital.

❑ Space between words   ❑ Ends with a period

WORD BANK

garden
grow
plant
seed
shovel
spring
sprout

✓ Check each sentence:

❑ Neat handwriting ❑ Starts with a capital.

❑ Space between words ❑ Ends with a period

WORD BANK

dark
ground
light
long
tunnel
under

✓ Check each sentence:

❏ Neat handwriting ❏ Starts with a capital.

❏ Space between words ❏ Ends with a period

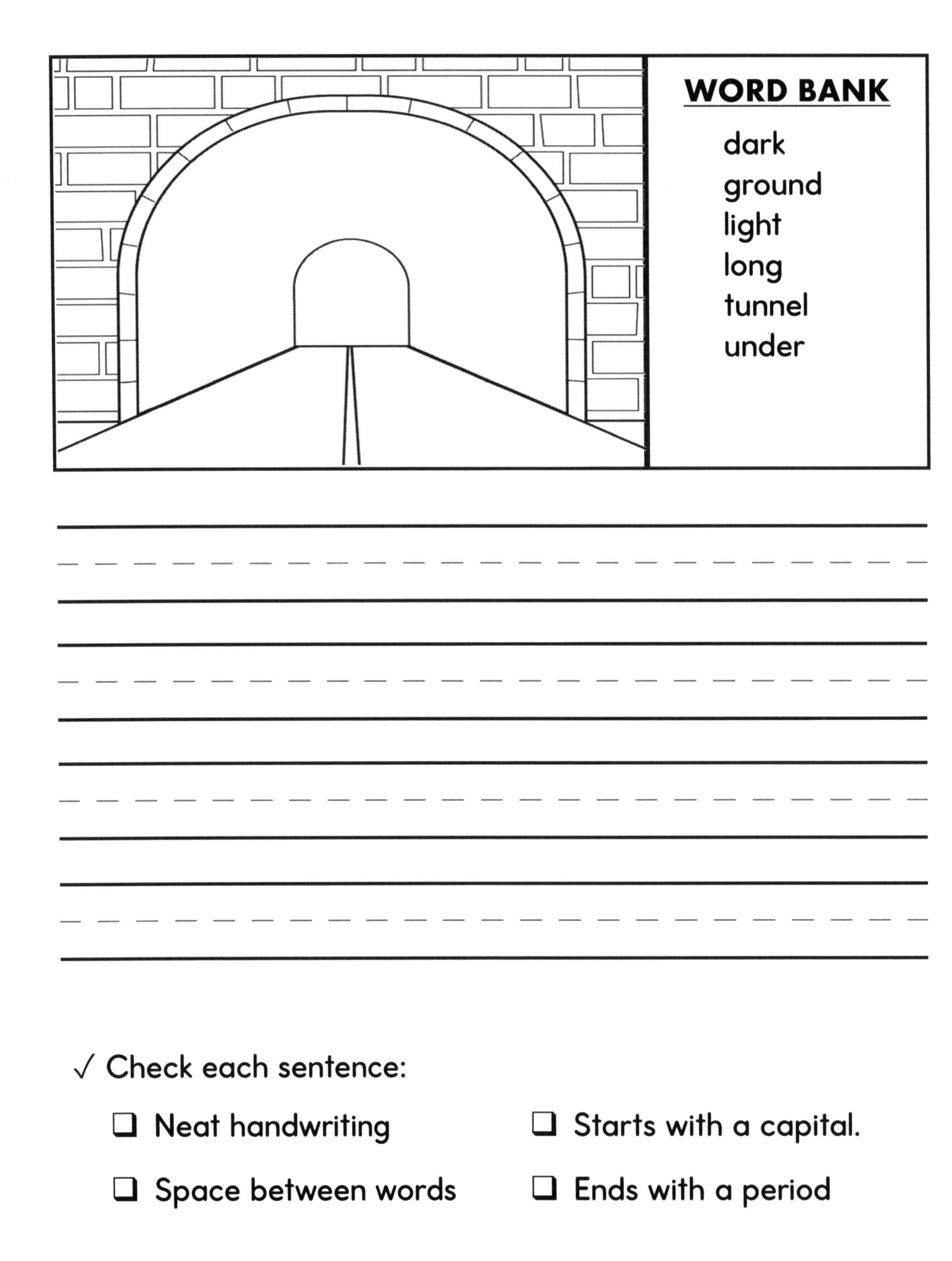

Made in the USA
Middletown, DE
26 February 2025